A Little Death

A LITTLE DEATH

Mary-jane Creel

VANTAGE PRESS
New York / Washington / Atlanta
Los Angeles / Chicago

FIRST EDITION

All rights reserved, including the right of
reproduction in whole or in part in any form.

Copyright © 1987 by Mary-jane Creel

Published by Vantage Press, Inc.
516 West 34th Street, New York, New York 10001

Manufactured in the United States of America
ISBN: 533-06997-1

Library of Congress Catalog Card No.: 86-90037

Let Haley Marie be as so many flowers . . . borrowed from God. If the flowers die or wither, thank God for a summer loan of them.

Contents

Preface ix
Acknowledgments xv

1. How to Help Yourself 1
2. How to Deal with Other Children 12
3. Taking Your Baby Home to Die 19
4. Deciding to Have Another Baby 32
5. Where on Earth Is God? 43
6. The Aftershock of Death 59
7. How to Be a Good Friend 69
8. Well-meaning People Who Say and Do the Wrong Things 76

Preface

"Nothing good comes easy. Nothing easy shows how good you are." This little quote has so much depth and truth in it, and it certainly applies to me. I never thought I would write a book; and yet, because of my daughter's illness and death, I have been compelled to write this book. The title of my book, *A Little Death*, has dual meaning. The "little" is referring to *little people* or to very young children or infants. Also, the title refers to the fact that when a child dies, a *little* part of the parents dies also.

The initial pain that resulted from my child's death was so terribly deep, lonely and overwhelming, that in essence it consumed my whole being. Therefore, I had little time, spirit, mood, feeling, or energy for anything except this deep pain caused by my loss. At first, I literally had to fight for every breath, and my body ached from the tension of coping.

There are many phases of grief that everyone seems to exhibit to a point, but the end results of this grief are *not* always the same or successful. Different people take different paths in order to resolve their grief; one very accessible and logical path is to read how others dealt with their loss. There are many books that deal with the subject of death, and I have read many of them. Some of the books were very healing and comforting, yet most of them do not deal with the core and depth of infant death (miscarriages, stillborns, and neonatal deaths). Most of the books that deal with infant death simply let the reader know that the problem does, in fact, exist. Of course grieving parents already know the problem exists and is very real. What they need are answers to questions and a means of dealing with the pain of their loss.

Many books miss the *fine* points of dealing with the differences between infant death and the death of older people. Infant death is not just bad, it is also *different*, because it simply does not follow the normal scheme of nature: people expect to outlive their parents, and they expect their children to outlive them.

Of course, a person is never *really prepared* for death, even when he has been told it is forthcoming. The untimely and sometimes unexplainable death of an infant carries such intense grief that it is often misunderstood by many people. The purpose of this book is to help those who are suffering from the loss of their infant to deal with the loss and reestablish themselves after such a loss. Also, the book is *aimed* at those who have not faced the impact of infant death, to make them aware of the intensity of such a loss and also to teach them how to be a soothing instrument in the healing process of grieving parents.

I must say that because of my experiences with my daughter's illness and death I have learned that life is not easy. I am sure it will not become easier, but I am also just as sure that my life is much richer and fuller because of my little Haley Marie. I want her life here on earth to have meaning to other people. Of course, she has meaning to me, but this book will give her life a real meaning to others. I want this to be a book that will help people get through and deal with the shattering loss of a child and not just another sad story. . . .

Mary-jane had been in labor for twenty-six and one-half hours, and she is now in the delivery room with her husband, Larry; her obstetrician; and two nurses. It is 3:07 P.M., Sunday, September 26, 1982.

OBSTETRICIAN: Push . . . one more time, Mary-jane.

LARRY: Come on, Mary-jane, you can do it one more time.
OBSTETRICIAN: It's a girl!
LARRY: Mary-jane, you've got your girl! Look at her!
MARY-JANE: What's the APGAR and how much does she weigh?
NURSE: She weighs three pounds and eleven ounces. The APGAR is six for one minute and nine for five minutes.
MARY-JANE: Why is she so small? Somebody, tell me . . . why is she so small?
LARRY: Hey, she's a little small but she has ten fingers and ten toes, so she'll be fine. . . . Just think . . . you've finally got the little girl you've always wanted.

Mary-jane and Larry have been taken to the recovery room, and it is approximately 3:45 P.M.

MARY-JANE: I can't believe it . . . but she's so small. . . . Why, Larry . . . why is she so small?
LARRY: You saw her . . . she's little, but she's got everything she's supposed to have. We might have to leave her here for a while until she puts on some weight, but we can handle that. . . . Just think, we have our girl. . . . I'm going to call your mother.

Later . . . Mary-jane's mother has come to the recovery room and the obstetrician enters . . .

MARY-JANE: Is she all right?
OBSTETRICIAN: I'd rather you wait and talk to your pediatrician.
MARY-JANE: Please . . . tell me the truth.
OBSTETRICIAN: I believe your baby has a genetic problem.
MARY-JANE: *(Silent, stunned, fading within herself)*: I'm all right . . .
MOTHER: Hey, don't borrow trouble. Just wait and see what your pediatrician has to say.

Later . . . in a private hospital room away from the maternity ward, the pediatrician and Larry enter the room.

MARY-JANE: What is it? Tell me. . . . What's wrong?
(*Larry begins to cry openly.*)
MARY-JANE: Oh God . . . please . . . what's wrong?
PEDIATRICIAN: Mrs. Creel, your baby is a trisomy-18. Your baby is going to die. There is nothing we can do for her.
MARY-JANE: Are you one-hundred percent sure? You could be wrong . . . right? Please, please . . . give her a chance.
PEDIATRICIAN: I'm sorry . . . I'm completely sure, but we will send a blood sample to Birmingham to verify her condition.

Then the doctor went on to explain Haley's condition as having three eighteenth chromosomes, whereas the normal baby has two of these chromosomes. He proceeded to tell me that Haley also had a severe heart defect caused by her genetic disorder. Her heart had a pronounced hole between two of the chambers, causing blood to back up into the lungs. He also told me the average life expectancy of a trisomy-18 was about two months, although some have lived as long as a couple of years. At this point, the doctors were not sure that she would survive the first night, or even go home.

Larry left to call his parents and to be with our two sons. The doctor told me he was going to bring Haley to me. I was terrified of seeing her because I thought she would look as if she were dying. Then I remembered that I had seen her when she was born. This puzzled me because she looked small but perfectly normal. My mind ran wild. . . . I thought someone must have switched my baby for someone else's, because my baby looked normal.

I will never forget when my doctor brought that tiny, little bundle into my room . . . gave her to me and left me with her all alone. I was petrified to be alone with her. She was all wrapped up so I could not even see her face. I sat there forever . . . wondering if I could take seeing a dying baby. She moved slightly and made typical baby sounds. I timidly folded back the soft blanket and saw her beautiful, perfectly normal, little head with soft brown hair. She was so pretty! I thought, *How can this be. . . . She looks so normal!* Then, I began to uncover her whole body and examine her all over, and still . . . she looked perfect. I wondered if what my doctor had told me could really be possible. I actually began to believe my doctor had made a terrible mistake. How could a baby be dying and yet look so perfect? It just did not make sense.

Haley had a rough first night in that she had to be suctioned and given oxygen several times. I stayed in the hospital nursery much of the night, watched as nurses worked with her, and rocked her myself when they would let me.

Haley made it through the night and managed to improve. The doctors moved her into my room, so I could learn to care for her properly. Haley and I went home in three days, and Haley's journey into our family life began. She gave me five and one-half of the most intense, rich, warm, full, heartbreaking, and loving weeks of my entire life. Haley touched my family's life as nothing ever had before or ever will again.

GOD, THANK YOU FOR SHARING YOUR BEAUTY.

Haley Marie Creel
September 26-November 4
(1982)

Acknowledgments

This book has become a reality only through the love and help of many people. Jean Johnson, Billy Ray Warren, Connie Walden, and Susan English spent many hours proofing, editing, and helping make my thoughts flow into the pages of my manuscript. Dr. Foster Eich, Dr. H. H. Floyd, and Dr. James Link gave endless hours of counseling, support, advice, and encouragement to make my book a source of healing. Their minds, hearts, and doors were always open to me. Alyce Pride and Marilyn Patterson, both of whom were constant sources of advice and suggestions, were nurses who saw the need for this healing endeavor for me as well as others. Most of all, I am thankful for my wonderful parents, Paul and Betty Yokley; my husband, Larry; and my sons, Kevin, Austin, and Daniel. They were always there for the tears, pain, and frustrations that were created by my loss and the need to write this book. To my mother, a special thank you for the long hours of typing and loving moments of encouragement.

I would also like to thank the following clergymen, for their spiritual guidance and wisdom, and for their permission to quote them in this book:

Hudson Baggett, Ph.D., editor of *The Alabama Baptist*, 3310 Independence Drive, Birmingham, Alabama, 35209, Baptist minister.

Wilbur Foster Eich, III, M.D., Doctor of Pediatrics, Methodist minister, Episcopal priest, 201 Flurnoy Avenue, Florence, Alabama, 35630.

Naaman Daly Goode, B.S. and M.A. degrees in biology, Church of Christ minister, 4708 Sparkman Drive, Huntsville, Alabama, 35801.

Thomas M. Phillips, Baptist minister, First Baptist Church, Killen, Alabama, 35645.

—Mary-jane Creel

A Little Death

1

How to Help Yourself

A bereaved parent must work at getting better after losing a baby. The first step is knowing and admitting the grief exists and recognizing that the baby is worth grieving for openly. "Support systems" are very important at this time. Be patient with the caring people who make up these systems. You must help them to help you! Do not feel that you have to put on an act for your friends. They may not totally understand your feelings, but they will try to be sympathetic with your anxiety and certainly be there in spite of it and, ultimately, because of it.

You must recognize your need to grieve as normal. I think most grieving parents think of themselves as crazy, and even that thought is perfectly normal! There is a wide range of normal feelings during the grieving process. Some of these feelings are very extreme and intense, and you may be fearful of some of these emotions. For example, I can vividly remember feeling very comfortable with the thought of dying. I actually felt that dying would be a welcome relief from all my pain. I tried to *think* life out of my body; I literally was trying to die from a broken heart. I also felt as if I could be with my little girl and that she needed me to take care of her. This state of mind really frightened me, because I have always felt only crazy people contemplate death. So, I thought I was actually losing my mind. I needed to find my reason for living. I really had to work to get myself out of this depression. I was so depressed, I feared for my life. Did you read that? I said I feared for my life. Hooray! I *really* did not want to die after all, and maybe I was not crazy either. Such irrational thoughts, as horrible as they may seem, will pass with time if you cultivate a positive attitude. Of course, I am the first to admit that this is not an easy task. I must emphasize that you have to work at being happy, even in ordinary circumstances; so, obviously, a tragedy requires all the strength you can gather.

Another fear was that things could be worse. People told me this a million times. This statement literally horrified me, because I realized it was true. The thought that something could be worse than watching my child die before my eyes was totally incomprehensible to me. It horrified me to think things could indeed be worse. I felt as if my life was totally intolerable, with the present situation, so how on earth could I survive anything more? That was a very despairing time for me.

Simply wanting to get through a particular situation will not make it happen. All the words in the world will not make the hurt go away. This book is full of words that, hopefully, will guide and help you to cope with the devastating impact of your loss. Yet, you, ultimately, have to be willing to help yourself. You can put the words to use by constantly repeating positive and meaningful ones to yourself, and you will soon be comforted by many of them. I can remember reading more books the first few months after the loss of my baby than I had read all through my years in school. I was groping around, desperately looking for the magic words and answers to make everything all right again. I was literally afraid of living.

Try not to dwell on things that cause you more pain. Dwelling on such things will only add to your suffering. Instead, you should concentrate on comforting, positive things, and these will pull you through.

You cannot expect the loss and hurt to disappear by itself. It simply will not happen. You should not expect other people to get you through all the intense grief that you are experiencing, without putting forth a whole lot of effort to help yourself. You must be willing to work harder than you have ever worked in your life to reestablish yourself. If something is worth having, you must work for it. I believe a fulfilling life is worth the effort! Of course, your family and friends can and will be a great deal of help, but they cannot do it without your being a willing receiver of their support. To be such a receiver, you must recognize your need not only to survive the loss, but also to come out on top of things once again.

Of all the feelings we have to deal with after the death of a baby, guilt is the hardest one to live with or to eliminate. My little girl was a trisomy-18, and there simply was no person or thing to blame for the disorder. For some reason, human beings must have a cause or reason for everything that happens, and I am certainly no exception. Therefore, I had to blame myself and take on the guilt. The question was: What could I feel guilty about, since there was nothing that could have prevented my baby's disorder or changed the fact that she was going to die? I decided I was being punished for wanting a little girl too much. I thought God was trying to tell me something or teach me a lesson. Of course, with time and rational thinking, I realized this was not true. Face it; a lot of people want a little girl as much as I did, and they get one. Why should I be punished and not them? I finally figured out that these trains of thought were self-destructive and absolutely not true. But, it took many months of hard work on my part to realize that I should not suffer from this tremendous guilt. It was pointless suffering, and it hurt me and the people who loved and depended on me.

There are several ways to overcome your guilt, depending on your reason for such feelings. In some instances it simply takes time to reorganize yourself and get over the initial shock, emotional numbness, and stress. This is usually the case when nothing human directly caused the death of the baby and nothing could be done to prevent it. Such situations could be genetic problems, congenital defects, sudden infant death syndrome (S.I.D.S.), or uncontrollable physiological problems. As long as you know that everything was done that was humanly possible to prevent the death, then the need to feel guilty will fade with time and reorganization.

In cases where the death of a baby is questionable in any manner, the guilt is much more difficult to overcome. Parents must learn to cope with this guilt, or the healing process will be unduly prolonged and possibly remain unresolved. You must not let the guilt consume you or remain dominant in your life for a prolonged period of time. If you find you cannot deal with it, then seek ways to overcome the problem. Give yourself time; but do not allow yourself to sink deeper and deeper into irrational thinking or you may find your situation unbearable. Sometimes an autopsy will clear up any fear concerning the cause of death. This procedure could eliminate the feeling that the mother did something wrong during the pregnancy. Another aid would be talking with your obstetrician and/or pediatrician to clear up any doubts about the situation. You should also consider some form of counseling on a professional level or speaking with a person who has had a similar experience. Never think of yourself as above needing or asking for help, especially if it could make the difference in being happy or sad for a lifetime. I have found that there are always relief and comfort in talking about your pain, especially with a person who has suffered a similar loss. Also, believe it or not, there is always someone worse off than you, and to some people this is comforting. The comfort comes from seeing the person deal with his tragedy and getting along well in spite of it. This gives you a feeling that if he can make it with all he has been through, then surely you can too.

It is important to understand your feelings of loss. A mother's hurt is much different from a father's. Usually, when a baby dies, society caters more to the mother's emotions than to the father's. I know a father hurts tremendously when his child dies but he probably will not show his emotions as readily as the mother. He will feel the pressures of society to be strong and stable, so he can take care of his wife. I honestly think he suffers as much from what everyone expects him to be as he does from the actual loss. He feels as though he is not allowed to vent his true emotions. Because of the father's behavior, the mother may feel as if he does not hurt as much over the loss of the baby as she does. She may even be angered and hurt over his apparent lack of feelings. The husband, in turn, is angry, because he does not feel that he can express his pain. This seemingly simple lack of understanding on the part of both parents can cause a real problem in their marriage. This is not uncommon at all. As a matter of fact, the death of a child places such stress on a marriage that severe problems often develop within a few months. Sometimes, counseling is needed for couples who cannot deal with the death.

    I can remember wondering why my husband did not seem to be hurting like I was. I thought either I was handling things badly, or, that he really did not care as much as I did. Nevertheless, I decided to ask him about it and I will never forget his response. He said, "You have enjoyed Haley more and, consequently, you are going to hurt more." My husband went back to work after we brought Haley home to die. I was the one who bathed her, fed her, rocked her, sang to her, and enjoyed her. I spent every moment of her life loving her. Because of my attentiveness to Haley and the fact that I had carried her for nine months and already had a bonded attachment to her, my husband felt I surely hurt more deeply. He did not feel the loss in quite the same manner as I did. We both could accept our grief as individuals *and* as a loving couple. Fortunately, Larry is a very understanding and caring man, and he allowed me to find my way through our loss. I realized he truly cared, but he expressed his feelings differently. Our marriage grew and became stronger because we loved each other and our baby.

After the problem of guilt is resolved or at least bearable, then comes the big "WHY?" This question tormented me more than anything else for months. It kept surfacing and spoiling any feelings of progress, as I was trying to recover from my loss. I felt that I was going forward two steps and then falling back one, all because I could not figure out "why?" Why me? Why my little girl? Why any child? Why do I have to hurt so much? Why did she or any child have to suffer and die? The questions concerning "why?" could have gone on forever and the lack of answers was just as endless. Even if there were no apparent answer, I needed to resolve it before I could get on with my life. I have discovered one thing in all my soul-searching, and that is the answer to "why?" The answer for me was, and still is, if God came down and sat with me in my home and told me why, I probably would not like the answer. I am sure I would want Him to find another way. To me, the answer might be worse than not knowing, because I believe any reason for taking my child is totally incomprehensible. So, I decided not to dwell on "why?" anymore, and I can accept not knowing the answer more easily than wanting to change it if I did know why.

I talked with my pediatrician about some of his encounters with dying children and their parents. The subject of "why me?" came up, and he said he had an answer. His answer was simply "why not me?" He said that every person thinks of himself as a special and unique individual, and that they do not think that bad things will or should happen to them. We think such things will only happen to *someone else.* Think about it for a moment. . . . You are someone else to everyone except yourself. So, why should you be any different and expect only good things to come your way? Everyone has his share of disappointments, and you are no exception. I will admit that I believe losing my baby was certainly more than a mere disappointment, but I am rational enough to also realize other people have a lot of heartache as well. I am sure others have many different types of hurt, but it is hurt just the same. It just so happened that my hurt took its form in my losing my child.

Any way that you look at it, the answer to the question "why?" is not going to be satisfactory. The real solution is to accept the situation, work your way through it, and resolve your grief. You cannot ignore the problem; instead, you must accept and resolve it and reorganize yourself.

Another hurdle to overcome, as you help yourself deal with your child's death, is the sense of failure. As a parent, you feel an overwhelming sense of responsibility to your children, especially to a helpless infant. You have instinctive feelings to sustain the baby, no matter what. I have always managed to gather all the strength necessary to pull my children through many difficult situations, such as surgery, extended hospital stays, extremely high fevers, choking, aspirations, and more stitches than I can begin to count. I have always prided myself in detecting their illnesses early enough to keep the really bad things under control. But, all of a sudden, I could do nothing to help my baby live; this left me with a total, absolute sense of failure. As Haley's mother, I regarded my role as where the buck ended. I felt that, ultimately, my responsibility was to figure out the way to make her better. I was not supposed to allow her to die. As with the snowball effect, I also felt as if I had failed myself, my husband, my other children, my parents, my in-laws, my friends, and the list can go on and on. My self-image was reflected in the show of disappointment in myself. I was actually angry with myself for allowing my child to die. I felt a lot of self-blame for not living up to the meaning of the word "mother."

Another phase you will face is the intolerable sadness you experience after the death of your child. I remember wondering if I would ever really be able to laugh again. I could not get the overwhelming hurt out of my mind. It seemed to plague me, and I wondered how other people got through a loss such as mine. I thought that something was wrong with me because I felt I had to grieve alone, just so others would not know how badly I handled everything. I actually looked forward to being alone during the day, so I could cry and not bother anyone. Then, when I was with my family and friends, I would concentrate on being strong and in control of my emotions. At times, my body would literally ache from the strain of trying to keep my composure. I wore myself out trying to be normal!

After wading through all the emotions of grief, I discovered that the key to survival was being positive. You will have your seemingly hopeless moments, but these will become less frequent and less intense. Most of your thoughts can be analyzed in two different ways, positive or negative. For example, I know a mother whose baby died from an infection due to the condition called spina bifida, or open spine. The little boy could not lie on his back because of the protrusion of the spinal cord. He was seven weeks old when he died, and his parents buried him lying on his back, because that was the normal procedure. Since then the mother has had anxiety concerning the baby hurting, because he is on his back. She still feels he would be more comfortable on his stomach. The positive approach would be to think how relieved the little boy must be now that he is free from pain, whole and normal. Actually, he is probably happy and proud he can lie on his back, like other children.

Try not to think how horrible it is that your baby has died but, instead, be relieved that he is free from suffering and pain. Be a better, stronger, and more-caring person because of your child. Try to live your life in a manner that would make your child proud that you were his parents. I truly believe I am a better wife, mother, daughter, daughter-in-law, and friend than I would have been without my experience of having Haley. She taught me more in her short five and one-half weeks on this earth than most people learn in a lifetime. She has been a positive addition to my life, and I am richer as a result of giving birth to her and sharing her life. Of course, I would like to believe I would be a good person without this shattering experience, but I know in my heart she changed my life, and I am better for it.

I realize it is hard to think positively and be patient when you are hurting so badly. Just keep in mind, reestablishment will come with time and effort, and you will make it. Even though your life will never be the same as it was before the death of your baby, it can be peaceful, hopeful, and cheerful again. I can remember when I cried most of the time and truly hurt 100 percent of the time. I can still look back and feel the great, intense pain, just as though I were living it all over again. The difference is that I can always bring myself forward to the present, which is filled with happiness once again. The grief does not dominate my days and nights, but it can still be recalled and felt. The loss of my little girl now has taken its proper position in my life, in my heart and in my memory. All of this will come with the resilient beauty of life!

Reflecting on my feelings after my baby died: At first, my mind did not really function, even on a simple level. I was very numb and dazed. My feelings were hurt very easily by things people said. The deep hurt seemed to, literally, *consume* me. The ache was always there, and I felt as if I could not stand the horrible grief. The pain was not just in my heart, it was engulfing my whole being. I remember wondering if I would ever be truly happy again. My heart ached so much that I am sure it would have registered on an electrocardiograph. But, the pain did not stop with my heart. It was much deeper, and I felt soreness throughout my entire body. It reached to my very soul. I felt as if my whole body, from head to toe, was hurting. I went through a week or so of hysterical crying and lost control of all my emotions. Then, I finally realized the crying did not make the hurt go away. It only accomplished wearing me out. I aged dreadfully during this time, both physically and emotionally. After I realized I was not getting better, the good old standby, logic, stepped into my mind. My thought processes were as follows:

1. Do I want to live or die? I decided I wanted to live.
2. Do I want to be happy or sad? Obviously, if I wanted to live, I wanted to be happy.
3. How can I ever be *truly* happy again? This question stumped me, at first. I was not really sure there was an answer for me.

Nothing occupied my time long enough to make me happy. Nagging thoughts consumed my mind. Why *my* little girl? Why do children have to suffer? How could this happen to me? Why are there no answers? I could not seem to progress to any degree. I think I knew all along that I *alone* had to get myself through and, yet, I was always searching for the miraculous cure. I finally realized that the cure was within my own spirit. I had to find the strength and courage to fight for happiness, within myself, and bring it to the surface. I had to figure out what it would take to make me feel good about myself and my life and then work toward that goal. My answer was to have another child. I finally found my true happiness, and it was worth every stressful moment that I had spent.

I have counseled many mothers who found some other solutions for their emptiness: adopt children, pursue a new career or hobby, write about their feelings, and help others by counseling, volunteer work, or public speaking. Keep in mind, whatever solution you choose, you will never be totally free from the memories of your baby. This is as it should be. You would never want to forget your child, but you do want to learn to live with the memories. I look at the loss of a child as if it were a wound that healed and left a distinct scar. If you have ever had a pronounced scar, then you know that particular area is rather sensitive at times, especially when touched or bothered. The same applies to your loss, in that your pain and suffering will leave scars on your heart. These scars will be sensitive at times. Sometimes, for no apparent reason, you will have a memory enter into your mind, or, maybe something you see or hear will stimulate a thought about your baby. This is perfectly normal, and how well you deal with this recall depends on how successfully you resolve and reorganize yourself during your healing process.

The last phase of the grieving process is resolution. You will recogize it, when you notice that you can be happy and feel good about yourself again. I have resolved my grief, and it is such an exuberant feeling, because I feel I have won the battle of a lifetime. I enjoy my progress, from a totally defeated person to the totally happy person I am today. It is a game to me to notice my growth. For example, I test myself to see how I will react in certain situations that might have upset me a few months ago. I know that my feelings do not get hurt as easily as they did earlier, and this is wonderful. I am truly glad I fought so long and hard to get happiness back. I honestly believe my life is better now than it has ever been, because I realize how terrifying it is to not be happy. Happiness is a word and feeling that I will never take for granted again. *I love happiness!*

2

How to Deal with Other Children

I believe if other children are involved when there is a loss of a baby, they present an especially delicate situation. From my own personal experience and from the experiences of mothers I have dealt with, I feel it is extremely important to be totally open and honest with the other children in your family.

Of course, the age and mental maturity of your children will determine the depth of their curiosity, their understanding, and their need to know about their loss. Even very young children will sense grief and sadness, and they will need assurance, even though they are too young to comprehend the total meaning of the situation. The main thing is to not leave them out, to the extent that their little minds and imaginations might draw harmful, fearful, or exaggerated pictures of the baby's death and cause them to carry a burden that could scar them for a lifetime.

Some children will initiate questions, and this is your opportunity to assure them that they are loved and that their world will not fall apart. If children do not ask questions, it does not mean their minds are not working and thinking about the death that has occurred. It probably means they are too afraid of finding out something bad, of upsetting their parents, or that they do not know what to ask to help themselves. In any case, they must be assured that the family unit is not falling apart because of the death, and that they are loved and needed more than ever.

It is very important to eliminate, as much as possible, the fears associated with death. The worst mistake made with children is to think they must be protected, by sheltering them from the truth. Their imaginations will, by far, cause them much more fear and anxiety than anything you could tell them about the death. It will be difficult to talk about the death with your children, but they will welcome your honesty as long as it is given in a loving and caring manner. Actually, it will be a relief to be able to talk about the loss openly, and it will prove to be positive therapy for the family unit. It will bring the family closer and make you stronger and more secure with your children. Always keep the lines of communication open.

Use discretion, as you thoughtfully and lovingly choose the ways to tell your children of the baby's death or approaching death. Let them know it is all right to cry and hurt over the loss. Try to anticipate and understand possible personality changes in your children. They may become noticeably moody, hostile, or withdrawn. Such reactions are completely normal for a limited period, but it should improve with time. Parents should be available and understanding during the transition period. Of course, I realize you are suffering, too, and this can be a difficult time. Keep in mind that parents are certainly allowed to cry and hurt during this time, because children need to know their parents feel the pain just as they do. Actually, you will be good for each other during this period of grief. Try to make the healing process work *for* the family and not against it. It can truly make or break your family unit. If you let them, your children will make the loss of the baby much easier. Other children are living proof that you are needed, loved, and successful human beings.

The concept of death is very hard to comprehend, even for adults. I remember wondering how I could help my children deal with death, if I had trouble dealing with it myself. Soon, I realized children have a remarkable rebound reflex, and they can accept things quite well if they are directed properly. In our situation, I decided to tell my children that it was hard for me, too, but that we would get through it together. The children felt better just knowing that I was willing to share my fears and confusion. This admission saved my family and me much anxiety and loneliness. This sharing process made me thankful for my children's very existence. In reality, they were as much help to me as I tried to be to them.

Children have an amazing innocence about them that sometimes allows them to bear a situation better than adults. Do not expect them to grieve as long and as intensely as you. At first, the death will have a pronounced position in your family's everyday lives. This should pass with time, and everyone will gain more perspective as the weeks go by. Do not allow the death to dominate your lives for too long. Your children should not be forced to grieve or made to feel guilty because they are happy again. Instead, they should be allowed to be happy and should be able to hold special, loving thoughts and memories concerning their baby brother or sister. Your children will suffer from a variety of fears and confusion, whereas you will suffer from a much deeper loss and emptiness that will probably take many months to resolve. Do not demand that they suffer along with you, but, instead, be thankful they can be happy and normal again. The loss of your child should have a meaningful place in all of your hearts and minds, but it should never be overpowering for extended periods of time. I believe parents may have to control their emotions around their children to some degree. At first, I felt I had to cry a lot; but, because I did not want to upset my children, I actually did much of my crying at times when they were not at home. I did not think it would be good for them to see me totally out of control; and, yet, I did cry with them, for the purpose of letting them feel all right about being able to grieve. If you sense their need to cry, you should let them know it is all right, and you can do it together. If you are very observant, you will notice (especially in young children) your children searching your face to see how they should respond! Children will be looking to you, just to find out what they should be doing. Sometimes, they do not know how they should feel, so they want their parents to show them. This is such a delicate time, and parents must show great wisdom in dealing with their children.

My sons, Kevin and Austin, were told about Haley's condition by my obstetrician and their pediatrician in the presence of their daddy and grandmother. They were told that she was very sick and probably would not live very long.

Kevin, who was nine when Haley was born, is very intelligent; in fact, he is in the program for gifted children at his school. He has also audited some courses at our local university. Because of his higher level of understanding, he was more aware of Haley's physiological situation. He understood her condition as well as any layperson could. The biggest concern I had for Kevin was that, because he was so advanced, I worried he might hurt more. In essence, he was a mere child trying to cope with the situation on an adult level. Also, he is an extremely sensitive person who feels hurt deeply. With all of this combined, I feared it would all be too much for Kevin to handle.

On the other hand, Austin, who was four, was not old enough to really understand Haley's situation. All he was capable of comprehending was that something very bad had happened to all of us. He could not really understand the impact that Haley was going to have on our lives. He seemed to need our assurance that we all would be together and all right again. I think his first fears were erased when I came home with Haley. He felt safe with me at home, even though we all knew Haley would die. He needed to know we would be a family again.

I remember the first encounter with Kevin and Austin the day after Haley was born. I had gotten little surprises to give them after the baby was born and had packed them in my suitcase as I prepared to go to the hospital. I wanted the boys to know I cared for them very much, and I did not want them to think our new arrival would get all of my attention or threaten their family positions. Kevin was really getting interested in golf, so I got him some optic orange golf balls. Austin had wanted football cleats, so I got him some little white ones. I remember thinking how clever I was, because I got the presents without anyone knowing it. I never will forget the salesman's face when I gave him a piece of paper with the outline of Austin's shoe on it and asked for some cleats that size!

Because things were really bad, I knew the boys would need to see me to make sure I was all right. The original purpose of our first meeting at the hospital after the baby was born had changed considerably, from simply wanting to assure them the baby would not take over, to a much deeper assurance that our family could survive the tragedy that had occurred. I remember going down in the elevator and meeting my sons on the steps at an old back entrance to the hospital. This was more private than the lobby in the front of the hospital. I was hurting so badly and needed to hold and touch my children. With my two beautiful sons in my arms, I truly wanted to live and be happy again. I can still remember their warm, soft, caring, innocent little bodies needing their mother's loving assurance that our lives would not fall apart. I needed them to need me and to give me a feeling of *success*. All three of us cried and held each other for a time. Then, I gave them their little surprises! They, like children should, got very excited over the prospect of playing with their new toys. For the moment, they laughed; and, then, of course, the reality of the situation crept in and took over; and we were sad due to our overwhelming, prospective loss. And so, we mourned. . . .

As I left my boys, I felt such loneliness, knowing that I would hurt by myself in my room. I really wanted them with me, but I knew they could not bear seeing me in such a state. I was relieved that they were children and could vent their feelings through play at home.

I stayed in the hospital with Haley a total of three long, trying days. During this time, I had to get myself together and adjust to the idea of taking home a baby that would drastically change all of our lives. Even in the deflated and drained state in which I found myself, I realized that I was going to have to deal with my two sons when I got home with Haley. Also, I felt this was not a time for trial and error. I knew I had to handle them correctly the first time or there could be undue harm done.

My husband and I decided to involve the boys as much as possible. We were completely open and honest with them, to make sure they had as little problem as possible with their sister's condition and death. I did not want them to fear death, because I wanted them to know Haley would be better off in a place where she would not suffer anymore. I did not want them to think she was in a dark, scary place, but instead that she was in a warm, loving place where she was whole. I made sure the boys were aware of her pain, to help them accept her death as a blessing for her. Knowing she was finally free from pain and suffering made it much easier for us to accept her death. As we all saw her decline, I would emphasize her distressful face to the boys, so they would recognize the obvious peacefulness on her face after death, as a comfort for their pain and loss. I wanted them to feel it was all right to miss her and want her back, but, at the same time to know that she was happier and whole in heaven. I stressed that we all would miss her, but that we wanted what was best for Haley. Because she gave us so much joy while she was in our lives, I wanted her brothers to know that we owed her the peace she worked so hard to earn, in heaven. We keep her alive in our hearts today with memories of her gentleness!

We encouraged Kevin and Austin to help feed, rock, bathe, and love Haley while she was with us. They enjoyed her so much that we actually had to limit the time they spent rocking her and had to alternate the times they fed her, just so they both could have equal time. The boys loved her so and enjoyed her to the limit! They made each moment with her count, and it all registered in their little hearts. I believe their lives are much richer because of their experiences with Haley.

The day before Haley died, we all were aware of her greater distress. I again made the boys aware of her struggle for life. She died in my arms that night, and I felt sure one of God's most special little angels had returned home. Fortunately, my boys did not see Haley actually die. We let them sleep through the night while we cried over our deep, consuming loss. The next morning, we got the boys up and told them that Haley had died. Kevin cried openly, while Austin was simply quiet and confused. I remember holding them and trying to prepare them to see her before we took her to the funeral home. I reminded them of her great pain from the day before, and I told them to see the great relief and peacefulness on her face. The boys held her, touched her, rocked her, and saw her peace. They realized she was better off, free from stress. I think that time with her was well spent, because they saw what we could never put into words. During the moments of holding her after she died, they were relieved for Haley. We all grew very close and grieved. Austin decided we needed to get her some pink flowers, and he insisted that we make everything pretty for her. We involved the boys in all the arrangements for Haley.

I know all the time we spent together during Haley's five and one-half weeks of life was tedious, but it was well spent, because we drew closer as a family. We grew to appreciate each other much more, and our need for each other became deeply special. We did not simply get through it all, we made it together as a loving family.

3

Taking Your Baby Home to Die

First of all, let me clarify that this chapter is for parents who have the option to take their baby home to die. Some parents clearly do *not* have this option, because their child's condition is too complicated for them to properly care for the baby at home. In almost every case, a dying child has complications *other than* the fact that he is dying. Depending on the circumstances surrounding a dying baby's condition, there are many possible extra complications the parents might have to deal with, such as:

1. Seizures: Some babies have seizures as a direct result of their disease or disorder.
2. Convulsions: Convulsions may occur because of things such as high temperature or other temporary physical disorders and, in the dying child, the results can be fatal or, at the very least, much more extreme than in a normal child.
3. Infections: A dying child is usually much more susceptible than a normal child to any type of infection to which he is exposed. Usually, the infection will also have a more profound impact on the dying child than on a normal, healthy child. Types of infections might include viruses, such as the flu or pneumonia, or surface infections, such as in the open area of the spine in the spina bifida child.
4. External physical deformities: Many terminal conditions are readily diagnosed, because of the particular physical

deformities that are present. Most deformities are common to the baby's disorder. On the other hand, some deformities are isolated and not directly associated with the child's condition. In either case, the physical deformities may require special attention.

5. Force feeding: This is usually used as a result of extreme loss of weight and the fact that the child does not seem to consume enough food to sustain himself. Force feeding involves putting a tube through the nose, down the esophagus to the stomach, and feeding the baby through the tube or performing a gastrostomy (a surgical opening into the stomach through the abdominal wall), requiring the blending of special formulas that can be drained into the tube entering the stomach.

6. Breathing difficulties: These can result from underdeveloped lungs or a defective heart. In some cases, the child will actually have to cry continuously in order to breathe. If the heart is defective, it can sometimes cause the blood to back up into the lungs rather than being pumped out of the heart, and this backup can cause a drowning effect. As death approaches your child may have Cheyne-Stokes breathing (commonly known as death breathing or still breathing). This is the cessation of breathing for a period of time; then breathing resumes, usually in the form of gasping. This type of breathing may repeat itself periodically.

7. Suctioning: This is necessary whenever any material, such as mucus or other drainage material, blocks the airway. Also, suctioning would be required in cases of aspiration.

8. Monitoring of the baby's body position: Because of the baby's lack of body control, the parents periodically may have to turn the baby to prevent bedsores. This is a common procedure for babies with hydrocephalus because the head is larger and heavier than normal.

9. Lack of the blinking reflex: Some babies cannot blink their eyes; therefore, the parents have to put lubricating drops in the eyes to keep them from becoming too dry.

10. Extreme temperature: The dying child is more likely to have a negative response to higher temperatures than a normal child. The dying child's body is not as capable of coping with the extremes as well as a normal child's body.

In many cases, the parents may have to actually learn how to do certain procedures that would normally be performed only by medical personnel, such as giving injections to prevent seizures, force feeding to prevent starving, and dressing areas such as the open spine in the spina bifida child. Because some of these situations are extremely difficult to deal with, some parents, with just cause, ultimately choose not to be a part of the child's dying process. Instead, the parents choose to leave the baby in the hospital or to place the child in an institution. Depending on the combination and severity of the complications that the child has, the doctors and the parents should *jointly* decide if it is plausible to take the baby home to die.

In some instances, the choice to take the child home to die will depend more on the willingness of the parents to take the child home than on the actual severity of the child's condition. This chapter is written to reinforce parents who can and want to take their child home to die, as well as to encourage the undecided, apprehensive parents, who have the option, to give it strong consideration.

The decision to take a baby home to die is a very personal one. To some people, a dying child would be impossible to cope with at home alone. They would feel more safe and secure if the child were in the hospital atmosphere; and, they would not have to watch the dying process. Some parents just simply cannot cope with a dying child. On the other hand, some parents would not have it any other way than to take the child home to die. Of course, the decision would depend a lot on the circumstances involved in each particular situation. Those who have dealt with a critical hospital situation, such as the intensive care unit, know how cold, sterile, and impersonal it is. My pediatrician said he would never *choose* to die in intensive care himself, and he would never *choose* it for a family member *if* he had any control over the situation at all. Again, let me emphasize that this is a very personal decision.

Parents should deal with the situation in the manner that is best suited for them and they should not be made to feel guilty or isolated for whatever path they choose. But, parents should *strongly* consider taking their child home to die. I have dealt with many mothers who have lost a child. I have also heard of and seen many different ways of handling the death of a baby. This would indicate that there are many acceptable ways to cope with a dying child. But, at the same time, I have heard many heartbreaking regrets. Hopefully, you will be at peace with your way of handling your loss. Believe me, it will be hard to take your child home to die (as a matter of fact, I do not believe there are too many things on this earth that are harder to do than to take your child home to die), but I do not believe it is nearly as hard as a whole lifetime of guilt, regret, and heartache. There has not been another moment in my life that has been as painful and heartbreaking as the moment my baby died in my arms; but, at the same time, it was also the most fulfilling and perfect moment for Haley and me, in that she needed me to be with her as she approached death, and I needed her to be in my arms, so I could know in my heart I did all I could do for her. I was there when she needed me the most; I needed to know that, in order to survive my tremendous hurt. My suggestion to parents is to consider your doctor's advice and follow your heart. You might try taking the child home first, and, if the situation gets too difficult, you can always put the baby back in the hospital.

I never considered leaving Haley in the hospital or putting her into an institution to die. I have always felt that I would want someone who loved me to be with me when I die. I knew that I loved Haley and that she needed the love and comfort of her mother while she faced the hard task ahead. I remember my pediatrician telling me to take her home and love, rock, and sing to her. And that is just what I did.

The hospital and my doctors prepared me for taking Haley home, by letting me take care of her for two days before I went home with her. She stayed in my hospital room in a waterbed bassinet with a heat lamp. She was so tiny and precious and, most of all, she was *mine*. I wanted to make her days here on earth as warm and loving as I possibly could.

I was very fortunate to have such humane doctors. My pediatricians were so supportive, and they encouraged me to take Haley home. They never considered using Haley for testing purposes or experimenting. One of my pediatricians told me he was always willing to inflict any amount of pain on someone if he had any reason to believe it would help; but, in turn, if there was no hope, such as in Haley's situation, he felt it best to simply love her and make her days as comfortable as possible. My pediatricians called periodically to check on how we were all doing. They always made me feel as if they were just a phone call away anytime, day or night.

I was scared beyond measure to take Haley home, and yet I knew it would be the best thing for Haley, my family, and me. As hard as it was to see my child die, I am certain it would have been worse to sit at home and wait for a phone call telling me she had died. I could not imagine sitting in my warm, cozy den, while my little girl was alone, dying in a cold hospital. I needed to know that I had done all anyone could possibly do to help her. Sure, I suffered and hurt immeasurably for five and one-half weeks, but I reasoned that five and one-half weeks of heartache were much better than a lifetime of regret. And I truly feel I would have always regretted letting her die alone, without her mother holding her.

Much of the time Haley was alive was pleasurable, because I truly enjoyed bathing, rocking, and especially dressing her up in sweet, pink, frilly things. She had her own bracelet, locket, and ring, and I dressed her as though she were going somewhere special each day, even though I knew I could not take her out and expose her to any infection or germs in the public air. She was the little girl that I had always dreamed of having. I have had my little girl, and no one can ever take that away from me.

I knew Haley's days were numbered; we were never sure how long she would live. At first I cried a lot, and then I realized I should make the best of the days or weeks I would share with her. I could always cry later. I realized that many people would think I was crazy, but I decided to plan all the final arrangements for Haley immediately and then put such arrangements aside until I would need them. I felt that, by doing so, I would have the presence of mind to avoid mistakes I might regret later. I was afraid that if I waited until Haley actually died I would make wrong decisions, because of the lack of time to plan and because of fragile emotions. So, I decided to make all the arrangements for Haley, put them behind me, and then simply enjoy Haley's life. I did not want to worry about anything going wrong. I wanted everything to be perfect for her. I have spoken with so many mothers who lost their babies before birth, at birth, or shortly after birth, and they never had the opportunity to take their babies home. I used to think they were lucky because they did not have to watch their child suffer and die. But, with time, I realized I was lucky, too, because I did get to establish good, loving memories, and I had the time to plan for no regrets.

I planned everything right down to Haley's position in her casket. She always slept with her head turned to the left; I wanted her resting in her casket this way, so she would be more comfortable. Of course, the normal procedure was for the head to be facing straight forward.

My parents, husband, and I chose cemetery plots. This was a difficult decision for me. It took three different visits to the cemetery before I could even get out of the car to look. It was just so hard to imagine my little girl being out there all alone. I used to look at a cemetery as a quiet, peaceful place, but all of a sudden it looked so different to me. As I looked around, all I could see was enormous pain. I thought, *Just think how many people hurt—just as I am hurting now and will hurt in the future—for each and every grave in this cemetery.* It was so overwhelming, it made me cry openly.

I chose a beautiful white, lace-trimmed dress and bonnet, pink lace-trimmed socks, and white lace-trimmed shoes for Haley to wear. Actually, I had chosen the dress for her before she was born. Of course, at that time, I had no idea she would not be all right, and I certainly did not know I would be burying my little girl in the dress, rather than taking her out in it to show her off.

I bought Haley a collectors' doll before she was born. I also buried this with her. The doll's name was Ursula, and she had a beautiful face with soft, pink braided hair. Her dress had flowers that matched the little pink flowers that were appliquéd throughout the lace on Haley's dress. Ursula was actually bigger than Haley, if you can imagine that. I felt as if Haley would need a friend, and Ursula seemed just perfect.

My mother helped me with some of the more difficult things, such as choosing the casket. I wanted something very feminine and soft. My mother chose the casket and made all the necessary arrangements with the funeral home. She discovered that baby caskets are not always readily available, especially in the style and color she chose. So I am glad I let Mother take care of this before we needed it. I just could not stand the thought of putting my little girl in a blue casket or oversized casket that did not suit her. You would be surprised how little things can bother or haunt you later if you are not completely satisfied.

I also asked my mother to dress Haley, because I felt I probably would not be able to bear to do it myself. If she had declined because of the same emotions as I was feeling, then I planned to ask a very close friend. This seemed more personal than letting some strange funeral director do it for me. I felt that

Haley's tiny size required a woman's gentle touch to get her slip, little diaper, and ruffles just right.

We had a picture made of my husband, sons, and me holding Haley to put in the casket with her. We wanted her to know she had a family here on earth who loved her very much.

Haley died in November, a cold time of year. I knew any flowers that she would get would probably die overnight from the frost. I also knew that we would have to wait until spring to get grass to cover that horrible, freshly dug dirt. So, I decided I wanted tiny, silk, baby-pink roses and English ivy for her pall. I knew the silk would withstand the winter weather and keep her grave from looking so bare and harsh. Again, the planning ahead was the best thing, because we had to special order the type of roses I wanted. The florist ordered the roses, made the pall, and held it for me until I needed it. With all of this planning behind me, I could enjoy Haley for the rest of her life and know that when the time came, everything would be perfect for "my littlest angel."

In many cases, where a child's condition is diagnosed as terminal, the definition of time is still not clear. I have known mothers who were told their child would live for several years, yet the child died in a matter of a few days or weeks. Also, I have known mothers who were told their baby would die within a couple of months, and the child lived to be school age. The doctors do not mean to torment parents; they are simply trying to give them an educated guess, and sometimes the guess is very inadequate. The point is, you are so lucky to have any time with your child, so do not waste a moment thinking about how many more moments there are to enjoy.

It is so hard to look at your baby and really know he is not going to live. You begin to wonder why it has come down to actually dying. Dying is something that happens to older people or only to young people as a result of an accident. And, yet, you are supposed to accept it, bear it, and, hardest of all, watch it occur. I remember thinking that I had never watched a bird or dog or any animal *in the process* of dying. All of a sudden I was faced with watching my baby die and, of all things, helping her do it. How does a person do that? I have helped my boys do everything that was difficult in their lives; so, I realized that I would have to learn to help Haley through the difficulty of living and then help her have a comfortable passing into death. I decided to put all my effort into loving Haley; everything else would take its proper place. This simple logic worked for me.

I would look at Haley for hours, trying to permanently imprint her face in my mind. I never wanted to forget her sweet, delicate face; her tender cry; her china-doll size, her baby smell, and the softness of her body as I held her.

It is, of course, impossible to remember such things, even if you try very hard. Thinking back to other important events in my life, I realized how many details are not very clear. So, I tried especially hard to work at remembering every detail about Haley. The solution was obvious . . . take a lot of pictures! I took pictures every day, of everything—pictures of Haley getting a bath, taking her bottle, the boys rocking her, the boys holding her, Haley crying, Haley in her swing, Haley sleeping, Haley wearing all of her pink, little clothes, her daddy holding and loving her, her grandparents holding and loving her, and anything else that involved Haley. My mother even got a professional photographer to go to the funeral home to take Haley's picture. I would not take a million dollars for any of my pictures of Haley, because they represent the beautiful memories of my little girl.

At first it was hard for me to see these pictures. She was so pretty in her lace-trimmed dress and bonnet. The pictures were so perfect, because they showed me how peaceful, happy, and content Haley was; and I knew I had helped her through the difficult task of living, so she could have the peacefulness of death. I strongly encourage taking pictures of your baby, even after death, because as hard as it seems at that particular time, you will desperately need the pictures later.

Another difficult task will be the procedure of having your baby pronounced dead. This can be a harsh, impersonal time; or, it can be made a warm, caring, and more-bearable time. If your baby actually dies at home, there will probably be four choices of procedures:

1. Go to the hospital emergency room and have your baby pronounced dead.
2. Take your baby to your pediatrician's office, and he will pronounce your baby dead.
3. Ask your pediatrician to come to your home and pronounce your baby dead.
4. Take your baby to the funeral home and have your doctor pronounce him dead.

Of course, the choice will depend a lot on when, where, and how the child dies. I strongly suggest asking your doctor to come to your home or to meet you at the funeral home. Your pediatrician will know about your situation and will probably make suggestions as he sees the need. He will help guide you to the best procedure and help you deal with your baby's death. I remember my pediatrician telling me that he was more *my* doctor now than Haley's, because he could help me whereas he could not really help Haley. He really worked at making sure I could deal with Haley's life and death. I remember that on the day Haley died he came to pronounce her dead; and, later that day, he called to see how I was doing and to ask me to come by his office the next week for a consultation. He again called the day she was buried to let me know he was available if I needed him and also to remind me to come to his office the next week to talk. He was always willing to set aside time for me just to talk and to answer any of my questions. As a matter of fact, he has been one of my main supporters in writing this book!

If you go to the hospital or the doctor's office, you will be exposed to questioning, filling out forms, and waiting. The atmosphere will be chilling and impersonal. You can take your time with your baby at home. It will be hard to deal with the harsh reality of your baby's death, but do not act too hastily. Believe me, you are never ready for your baby to die, even if you have had weeks or years to prepare. It is much harder than you have ever allowed yourself to imagine. Your baby deserves these precious moments and loving goodbyes. You will always be glad you held and loved your baby after he actually died. Do not make the mistake of rushing this most valuable time.

Another decision you will need to make will be whether or not to let a funeral director come get your baby or to take your baby to the funeral home yourself. This decision, like all the others, will depend a lot on the situation. For example, if you have other children at home, I think, it would be best if they do not have to see a stranger coming into their home and getting their baby brother or sister. Such action might make them feel uncomfortable and scared for the baby. The funeral home personnel usually come to the home carrying a large bassinet-type basket to put the baby in. According to mothers I have talked with, it is devastatingly hard to give up their baby to a cold, strange man carrying a basket. Therefore, I recommend, if at all possible, that the family take the baby to the funeral home.

Haley died at 5:30 A.M., after a night-long fight with death. My husband and I waited until 7:30 A.M., to call our pediatrician. Dr. Eich had expected our call, because he had seen the distress and decline in Haley's condition the day before. He told me to take my time, and he would either come to my house or meet me at the funeral home. I called my parents to come to be with my other children, my husband, and me, before we took Haley to the funeral home. We all shared in telling Haley goodbye. Each one of us held and rocked her for the last time. My father stayed with my two sons, Mother went to get the pall and Haley's clothes and doll, and my husband and I took Haley to the funeral home. Riding in the car to the funeral home really felt strange—lonely and heartbreaking. I remember all the traffic and wondered why everyone seemed to be in such a hurry. What could be so important to all those people in the other cars? I wondered what they would think if they only knew my baby was dead in my arms.

I can still see the funeral director holding out his arms to take my little Haley. I just could not let her go that easily. I cried. . . . And I asked him if he was a nice man. Fortunately, he was very understanding, so he invited us into his office so we could talk. We talked about unimportant things such as the weather! But, he knew I needed the time to let go of my little girl. When I realized he was indeed a very kind man, I asked him to take her and keep her safe until my mother arrived to dress her. He gently took her in his arms and assured me he would keep her warm and safe until my mother came.

Because of all my previous planning, everything went smoothly and perfectly. I can honestly say, without any reservations, that I do not have any regrets concerning the arrangements for Haley and the way we dealt with her life and her death. There are several reasons for my contentment. I planned the arrangements ahead of time, when I had time to think about them and time to work my way through them. I had a wonderful mother, who helped give me distance from the situation, yet who was close enough to do things for me that I could not do for myself, such as choosing the casket and dressing my little girl. I had understanding doctors, who encouraged me to follow my heart, and who were always there to check Haley and give me support. I had a strong support group, A.M.E.N.D., that introduced me to a particular friend who had also taken her baby home to die. She called periodically to check on me and always had an understanding ear. One of the more important reasons for my having no regrets was my loving husband and sons. They wanted and needed to have Haley at home as much as I did.

But, as in all tough decisions in life, the success of my situation depended heavily on my own strength. I must say that I am proud of my part in the decision to bring Haley home to die, because I made it work for myself as well as for my whole family. I remained strong when it really got rough at the very end and everyone else was ready to put Haley in the hospital. Even my doctors were fearful that I might not be able to bear it any longer. They suggested I put her in the hospital, not because they could help her, but so I would not have to be alone when she died. I said, "No, I am going to do it right for Haley, and God is going to help me do it."

She and I fought with death all night, and I must admit by the next morning I was wondering if I could take it any longer. But, with great exhaustion, Haley and I made it together. The last person she saw before she died was her mother, the last thing she heard was, "Mommy loves you," and the last sensation she had was being held and rocked by a mother who loved her dearly for the five and one-half weeks she lived. Haley and I made it together. . . . She earned her place in heaven, and I earned peace of mind knowing I helped her get there.

I visit with Haley each day in my thoughts! I honestly do not fear death anymore, because I know I will see Haley again and she will be whole and normal. Some of my favorite people are children, and I certainly cannot imagine heaven without children. Heaven certainly seems much closer now.

One of my friends sent me this word of comfort after Haley died:

> Let her be as so many flowers . . . borrowed
>   from God.
> If the flowers die or wither, thank God
>   for a summer loan of them.

4

Deciding to Have Another Baby

In cases where parents have lost a baby, the decision to have or not to have another child is usually discussed. The decision to have a baby is very important under normal conditions, and this decision becomes even more intense when a baby has already been lost or when the possibility of losing a prospective child exists. The idea of being pregnant and having a baby no longer seems simple, ordinary, and the normal thing for a woman to do. It becomes *the mountain* rather than a simple molehill. All of a sudden life becomes so complicated and confusing. You will long for the simple, carefree days before all the tragedy of losing your child came into existence. But, the reality of the situation does exist, and it cannot be changed. However, you can partially rectify the wrong that has occurred.

As you will realize through your healing process, your need to survive and be happy again will become very pronounced. The obstacle that will constantly present itself will be whether or not to try again to have another child. Parents must not make the decision to have another child, or not to have another child, because of their tremendous initial hurt. I can remember my obstetrician telling me to give myself time to make a rational decision, rather than a distraught, emotional decision. Some people immediately say they will never have another child and, unfortunately, make the mistake of arranging some type of permanent birth control. Then later, when they have resolved some of their pain, they may wish they could have another child. As a result, their decision to permanently insure their not having more children becomes a source of guilt and bitterness. Consequently, the parents often regress to the initial loss. The point here is: The husband and wife should not rush into any decision until they can think clearly enough to give the situation proper attention. Clear thinking will come *only* with time.

Also, some women get pregnant too quickly. Often, they are really not ready to face another pregnancy, because they have not allowed themselves enough time to grieve and resolve the loss. This can cause a lot of unnecessary anxiety for the parents. Even a good pregnancy is not an easy task, so adding extra stress can make the pregnancy almost unbearable. So, the couple must use common sense and take the time to make the right decision.

Besides the need for some time to pass, there are many other factors that are involved in making the decision of whether or not to have another baby. Some of these factors include the mother's physical condition, her age, both spouses' feelings, other children, the parents of both the husband and wife, and certainly the possibility that something could go wrong again. Any one of the above factors can control your decision. For example, your physical condition could be such that you could not have another baby. If this is the case, and you do want another child, I highly recommend adopting a child. You could go through an agency or by way of a private adoption. An agency might take quite some time in getting a baby because of long waiting lists. A private adoption usually takes less time and allows the parents to be more selective of the parents and child involved. I would suggest getting on an agency waiting list while trying private adoption. This course would help cover all the bases. Of course, you will need to consult with lawyers, physicians, and hospitals.

Usually several of the already mentioned factors will enter into making your choice of whether or not to have another baby. The combination of factors will depend on the particular situation that exists.

Age is a factor usually considered by mothers over thirty-five years old. It seems that more problems exist for mothers in this category. For example, the percentage of babies with genetic defects rises drastically for mothers over thirty-five, thus establishing the need to consider genetic counseling and the possibility of certain tests such as the amniocentesis. Time is very important to mothers who have waited until their late twenties or early thirties to start a family. When a couple finally decides to have a child and loses one, they are faced with the possibility of running out of the necessary time to have the number of children that they planned. So, age can certainly affect the timetable involved in planning a family.

Another factor to consider is the feelings of your spouse. The loss of a child can certainly place a devastating strain on a marriage. Because of this, everything that is done as a result of the loss should have a positive effect in order to strengthen the relationship. Try to make the decision concerning another baby together. Search out the true feelings of your husband or wife. Make sure your final decision comes as a result of a joint effort and that you both really can live and be happy with the outcome. If you cannot seem to agree, then try to explain your feelings to each other and understand each other's views. Surely, through loving and caring, you will agree or at least compromise and come to your decision. It is extremely important to have each other's firm support in such a significant decision.

If you have other children, they should also be involved in the decision about another baby. They may not be old enough to express their opinion, but they should be considered since they have a lot of confusion to deal with because of the baby's death. They may fear more hurt as a result of having another baby. They may think the new baby will die also. So, parents must be prepared to deal with their other children's feelings with love and understanding. After all, their little world has been shaken as it never has been before, and they need to know it will stay intact for the duration. If the decision is made to have another baby, then you must reinforce your other children throughout the pregnancy, so they will feel comfortable expecting another baby brother or sister.

Sometimes your parents and in-laws present a special problem during the process of considering another baby. They may have very strong feelings about whether or not you should try to have another child. They will probably base their decision on the same factors you base yours, and yet their answer may not be the same. This does not mean your answer is necessarily wrong, but you should consider their opinion and give more thought to your decision. If you still feel you are right, explain your feelings to your parents and in-laws and ask for their much-needed support, even if they do not fully agree with your choice. They, in turn, should respect your decision and be supportive. They should not harbor bad feelings because you chose not to agree with them. Your parents should recognize that you are responsible adults, even though they might still think of you as *their baby*. Be deserving of their respect by giving a lot of thought to your decision and covering all possibilities. A misunderstanding between you and your parents would only cause more stress where the situation is very difficult and strained already. The support and togetherness of your family will ultimately pull you through this otherwise unbearable time.

My parents were profoundly against my having another baby. They felt that my other two children should be enough for me. I never felt as if my two sons were not enough, but, in fact, they were more than enough in many respects. However, I did not feel the two situations were related, in that I did need to have another baby. This need had nothing to do with my love and need for my other children.

I did not want *to want* another baby, because I knew it would be much easier if I could simply put it all behind me and let it go. But having another baby seemed like the only answer for me. I actually tried *not* to want another baby, but I got nothing except extreme frustration and regression to the pain of losing Haley. I needed another child, because that is what my original goal was before I lost my little girl.

Fortunately, my parents did ultimately support me in my decision to have another baby. Even though they were initially against my having another child, they tried to understand my position, and they willingly and lovingly supported me. I, in turn, realized their apprehension was based solely on their love for me. I knew they just wanted to protect me from the possibility of more hurt.

As we all discussed our possible choices, we all realized we wanted the same things. We all needed to be together and happy again. The problem was that we had different solutions to the same problem. The key to my survival was knowing that my parents loved me and respected my judgment enough to trust me with the decision that would affect all of our lives. They let me make the right decision for me, and ultimately it was the right thing for all of us. I realize it must have been one of the hardest things for my parents to do. It takes really special parents to know when to let go and to hope they have raised their children right!

As for my in-laws, I never will forget what my mother-in-law told me concerning another baby. She said, "We'll be here and understand whatever decision you make." They were loving enough to be there for us, good or bad, and I really needed her to tell me just that!

As I worked my way through the initial pain and despair to arrive at my final decision to have another child, I knew I had three possibilities to consider:

1. To not have another baby;
2. To get pregnant and have to face the possibility of losing another child;
3. To get pregnant and have a normal, healthy baby.

I owed myself and my family a totally comprehensive decision. I considered and studied each of the three possibilities thoroughly.

First of all, I considered not having another baby. I tried very hard to like this choice, because it certainly seemed to be the easiest answer. The more I fought to *not* want another child, the more apparent it became that I needed another baby. So, although the choice of not having another baby was the easiest, safest, and most logical, it was not the answer for me. I truly felt we all needed a normal, healthy baby. After all, this was our goal before Haley was born.

The second possibility was to get pregnant and have to face the possibility of losing another child. Obviously, this possibility required a very close and intense investigation. I really did not want to think of this situation at all. But, because the possibility existed (actually the odds were increased), I had to think about it and face the fact that I could lose another baby. A second loss would be totally devastating, but I had to take the chance. I admit, at times I felt as though nothing could go wrong again. I felt I had paid my dues and had already suffered my share of hurt in this lifetime. But, when I met some mothers who had lost two babies, it shocked me back to reality. It can fail again. Of course, I was banking on having a healthy baby. I had to try. . . . I remember thinking, that if I did have a normal, healthy baby, it would save my life and in turn my family's happiness. And, if it failed, I would give my little Haley someone to be with in the cemetery and heaven. Either way, I could not be all wrong.

I had personally experienced having a child "born dying," and I searched my soul to determine if I could indeed face this very real possibility again. I remember how I felt the pain my child felt as she steadily declined, and it was overwhelming. To face this again would be a very difficult and heartbreaking path for me to take. All I knew at this point was that I was not doing well without my baby, and even if I failed again, it would not be as bad as not trying at all.

Of course, I realized losing another baby would have engulfed me with sickening force, but I had to trust in God and hope it would not come to that end. So, although I felt the decision was hard, I also felt it was the best choice for me and my family. At this point, I prepared myself to face another pregnancy, and I set my goal to have a normal, healthy baby.

After dealing with possibility numbers one and two, I dreamed of possibility number three: to get pregnant and have a beautiful, normal, healthy baby. This seemed like such a fantasy and the ultimate solution to remedy the emptiness from losing Haley.

I did get pregnant, and I set the goal of having a normal baby. At first, I must admit I was depressed at finding out I was pregnant again, because it brought out the distinct fear of risking all the hurt I had endured after Haley died. I felt as if I were letting myself in for the unbearable pain all over again. But again, I had to collect myself and deal with the situation at hand, which was getting through another pregnancy.

After I adjusted to the idea of having another baby, I busied myself with redoing the nursery; this really occupied my time until I had to go for my amniocentesis test. I had such mixed emotions about this test. I feared the results and also the small possibility of losing the baby because of the test. But, as I reminded myself, the test was a part of the deal of getting pregnant. I had made my choice when I decided to have another baby, but it all seemed a little harder to actually go through with the plan.

The trip with my husband to Birmingham Genetic Laboratory seemed totally insane. Although I knew I was too far along to back out now, I kept asking if I could really go through with this. I felt completely out of control of my destiny and at the mercy of life, God, and the geneticists. I was *afraid*.

I must say that the medical people at the test center were absolutely fabulous, very positive and reassuring. Still, I remember thinking, *Is it worth all the worry and torment and what if it is all for another dead child? Could I take another loss? Probably not. . . .* One mother I talked with told me not to get my hopes up too high because, even if my baby was all right, I would still have that devastating emptiness over the loss of Haley. I thought surely I would not have to go through all of this and still not be any happier. The mother was wrong because having a normal, healthy baby did make everything much better. Of course, Haley will always have a special place in my heart, but Daniel filled my empty arms.

I remember the relief I felt after the test was over. I was calm and collected until I walked out of the building. Then I broke down and cried openly. My husband said candidly, "What are you crying about? The hard part is over." I was crying from relief. I was so glad it was over for the time being. I had been strong through the whole scary ordeal, and I just could not keep up the pretense any longer. I just let go and cried because I was so relieved and glad this big step was over. It was certainly a milestone in my pregnancy, and I had survived it.

The next step was getting the results. It took three long weeks for the preliminary results and four weeks for the final results. It was certainly one of the longest months of my pregnancy. My obstetrician called me and read the results. I was so relieved that everything, up to this point, was perfectly normal, that I cried as he talked to me on the telephone. He called again a week later, read the final results, and also told me I was going to have a male baby! Another beautiful little boy! I actually felt safe and relieved, because I knew I could have normal boys. I feared losing another little girl, but I felt very comfortable having another boy. I almost had the feelings of my younger son, that all little girls die. I honestly believed that I could not carry a little girl, which is intellectually ridiculous; but my mind was operating on a low enough level that sometimes I felt as if this were the case for me.

The next months were filled with facing the possibility of something going wrong at delivery. I got very edgy, as though I did not want to have the baby. I actually felt safer pregnant, because as long as the baby was inside of me he was safe. Because of my dealings with mothers who have lost babies, I have learned that a lot of babies are lost during the labor and delivery.

I had been pregnant for almost two years because I got pregnant three months after Haley was born. Believe me, I was weary. I was getting to the point of total physical and emotional exhaustion. I started having labor five to six weeks early, which scared me, because I knew it was too soon. Nevertheless, Daniel was on his way. I remember begging my obstetrician to put me to sleep, because I was so afraid of seeing something wrong. Of course, he would not do that; so he reassured me that things would work out. I was persistent about being afraid to see my baby, so my doctor suggested that I just keep my eyes closed!

My labor was relatively easy, but the delivery was very long, because Daniel was still high and he presented himself in a posterior position (face up). I remember pushing and pushing and pushing . . . in my mind I feared fetal distress because of all the pushing. I kept my eyes closed tightly as Daniel was born. Everyone in the delivery room wanted me to see him, but I just could not get the courage to open my eyes! This fear never really left me . . . it seemed to echo throughout the pregnancy, and it was even more intense at delivery.

I kept asking about the umbilical cord. I wanted to know if it looked all right because Haley's umbilical cord was the first thing that had keyed the doctor into knowing something was wrong. My doctor could not understand why I wanted to know about the cord, but I did not want to see Daniel. He delivers many babies, so he had forgotten about Haley's cord being so small and short. He just laughed, held up the cord for me to see, and asked me if I thought it looked all right! For something that is normally thought of as unpleasant looking, that cord certainly looked beautifully normal to me!

Even though everything seemed all right, I knew Daniel was small and premature. I feared he could not make it because he was so early. I constantly quizzed the nurses in the recovery room about Daniel's condition. They did not give me satisfactory answers, because they were busy working with him, making sure he was all right. Time seemed to stand still. I became paranoid and felt as if the nurses were keeping the truth from me. I needed them to tell me he was okay. I remember telling my husband that I thought they were lying to me and that I would know for sure when they took me to my room. I had been put in a room away from the maternity ward when I had Haley, so I knew if the nurses put me in the same area of the hospital again, something was wrong. I felt wonderful when they pushed me down the hall, turned to the maternity wing and put me in my room. I knew I had finally made it, because I was in the maternity ward! When the nurse started to leave, she laughed and said, "Now do you believe your little boy is all right and that we have not lied to you?"

It was not an easy pregnancy, emotionally, but it was well worth every tedious moment. If I ever had any doubts about the existence of God, they were all erased when I first held my little boy, Daniel. All my doubts and fears faded when I touched, smelled, felt, and loved him. His birth made me whole again. As much as I had hurt when Haley died, and during the months after her death, Daniel counteracted the pain with such tremendous joy. He changed my life. I think I truly realized, much more than the average mother, how precious the life of a child really is. Daniel made me believe in everything good again. What a great feeling!

It does not necessarily take a brave person to do what I did; I do not think courage enters into such a decision as much as the need to survive does. I am still somewhat awkward around my obstetrician, because he has seen me at my worst. He knows what a coward I really am. Most people think I am strong, but he knows how I begged to be put to sleep and not face everything. He knows the times I cried during my routine checkups. What most people do not understand is that it is not necessarily brave to go through something like this. People could say I was too much of a coward to face life without another baby. Or they could say I was brave and strong enough to do what had to be done. Whatever the case, another beautiful baby has blessed my life!

5

Where on Earth Is God?

I believe that parents' religious convictions or *lack* of them become very important when a child has died. God's role in their lives needs to be positive and reassuring rather than destructive or threatening.

My parents, my church background, and life in general never prepared me for such a shattering heartbreak as my child dying. It is sometimes hard for parents to know what to believe or think when such a traumatic experience occurs. Most people are totally unprepared when such an unnatural death happens. After all, we certainly expect our children to outlive us.

My first big question was, "Where on earth is God in all of this madness?" I knew I had not done anything bad enough to warrant such punishment, and yet I wondered "why?" I also thought of many people who seemed to deserve punishment much more than I, but their lives seemed free from tarnish. Of course, I do realize that everyone has his own hurts and heartbreaks; but at the same time, I feel many of them are self-induced. We bring so many of our troubles upon ourselves. But, as I learned by having Haley, such is not always the case. I took great pride in taking care of myself during my pregnancy. My doctors even went so far as to say, because of Haley's condition, I should not have been able to carry her full term. I should have lost her very early or at least by the second trimester. They felt, because I had taken such good care of myself, Haley was carried full term. The real shock is that she is the only child out of my five pregnancies that I have carried full term. It is as if I actually went beyond the normal precautions to prevent an unhealthy child, then nature turned all my positive efforts around and actually worked against me. With all my logic and educated reasoning, I could not see a practical reason for what had occurred. In other words, I felt as if I had been singled out for some reason. For all practical purposes, there did not seem to be a plausible explanation for the *mistakes* in Haley's karyotype; so, I kept going back to God. So, what could I say other than, "Where, indeed, is God in all of this madness?"

I had never considered myself an *overly* religious person, but I did think I knew what I believed about God. Had I been believing in the wrong things all these years? Did I lack depth in my faith? What had I missed, and how did I find it now? The unknown answers, the unsolved mystery, and the untimely death seemed to drain my faith and leave room for so much doubt. Ultimately, I was left with many questions, and that is why I chose to include this topic in my book. I put together several questions and statements concerning God that are commonly asked by or said to bereaved parents, and I sent them to ministers representing different denominations. Hopefully, their responses and thoughts will help clear up many misunderstandings, misinterpretations, ideas taken out of context from the Bible, and also serve as a comfort for your grief.

1. *Are my sins being reflected in my children?*

This is a commonly held belief today especially among people who have never suffered a painful loss or had a real reason to think about why bad things happen to people. I am sure I have thought that certain people have *deserved* their misfortunes from time to time; and, in turn, I have often wondered why certain, fine people have had to experience tragedy. Losing Haley literally shook my soul and made me wonder what on earth I had done to deserve such intense pain. I do not ever remember consciously thinking people's sins were reflected in their children; but, apparently I believed it to an extent, or I would not have felt that I was being punished through Haley's death. I had to find some explanation for this punishment. I felt that I was being punished, but I did not know what I had done wrong. In most cases, a person knows that he has done something wrong, and he expects the consequences or punishment. All of a sudden, I was being *punished*, but, as far as I knew, I had done nothing terribly wrong. Now, of course, I realize there is a large element of randomness to events and that God surely sends sunshine and rain on the evil and on the good alike. This concept is supported by Matthew 5:44–45. Some people think that all sickness and suffering result from sin; but the book of Job refutes this belief. The story of Job makes it clear that he was a *righteous* man, but that he suffered all kinds of tragedies in his life, including the loss of his entire family.

Ezekiel 18:18–20 makes it very clear that each person is punished for his own evil and only for his own evil. Verse 20 states, "The son shall not bear the iniquity of the father, neither shall the father bear the iniquity of the son."

I personally do not think punishment, sin, or right and wrong are the issues when a child dies. In John 9:1–3 there is a story about Jesus healing a man who had been blind since birth. "His disciples asked him, saying, Master, who did sin, this man, or his parents, that he was born blind? Jesus answered, Neither hath this man sinned, nor his parents: but that the works of God should be made manifest in him." This story indicates a much more meaningful purpose for a child's defect and/or death than merely a form of punishment.

Life would be simple if the good were always rewarded and the evil always punished, but it is just not that simple. Based on both scripture and my personal observations, a child's defect and/or death have nothing to do with the sins of the persons involved.

2. Will I know my baby in heaven as my child and will he know me as his mother?

The Bible does not tell a lot about what heaven is like, so I think heaven has a different meaning to each person. What might be heaven to one person might not be to another. Actually, I do not believe we are fully capable of understanding or comprehending what heaven will be like. Dr. Foster Eich, my pediatrician, and an Episcopal priest, had a very candid comparison to our lack of understanding about heaven. He said it would be like telling a three-year-old what sex is like between two people that truly love and care for each other. The child just has no means of relating it to his own experience. Is sex like chocolate candy? Is heaven like a feast? Yes . . . but it is much more than a feast, just as sex is more *pleasurable* than even chocolate candy!

I Corinthians 15 indicates that we will know and be known in heaven. This means that we will recognize and be recognized by our friends and loved ones. Also, there is reference to "the resurrection of the body," but it does not mean that we will have our earthly bodies with all the allergies, body aches, arthritis, and toenail fungus. Instead, in I Corinthians 15:15–57, Paul says we shall be raised with a "spiritual body." "As we have borne the image of the earthly, we shall also bear the image of the heavenly." We will not be as we are here on earth, but we will have a likeness that will be recognizable as ourselves. The account of the rich man and Lazarus in Luke 16:9–31 teaches that there will be knowledge and memory in the life hereafter. Notice especially verse 25, where the rich man is asked to remember things about his earthly life. Also, in the Old Testament, King David grieved about the death of his child and said that, since the child could not come to him, he would look forward to a reunion with the child, indicating that King David would know his child in heaven. People usually try to comprehend heaven by thinking of it in terms of the things they love most in life. Accordingly, I think of heaven as seeing my little Haley, whole, normal, and happy, and also of knowing her as my little girl and of her knowing me as the loving mother who cared for her on earth. I personally cannot imagine heaven without children. I certainly believe I will know Haley, and I will surely know I am in heaven when I see her there!

Rev. Tom Phillips, a Baptist minister, also thinks that we will all know each other in heaven but *not* in the same manner as here on earth. But, he further believes that knowing each other in the earthly manner will not be important. In other words, such knowledge will not be one of our priorities, in that other things will become more important and take precedence. The way I see this is that if it is not important to know my family when I get to heaven, that is fine; but, for now, it is essential for me to believe I will know my loved ones, especially Haley, because I need to see and know she is happy and normal. In any case, I do believe I will be satisfied with the way God has handled it when the time comes.

3. *Will my baby be whole and normal in heaven?*

There is no doubt in my mind that Haley or any other suffering child will be whole and normal in heaven. After all, heaven would not be heaven if we were suffering or unhappy. In I Corinthians 15 Paul says the "mortal shall have put on immortality." Then he uses the analogy of the seed, by saying that unless the seed dies or is put in the ground and dies, new life does not come forth in the form of the plant. This passage indicates that the resurrected body will be *different* but *real*. Also Revelation 21:4 tells us that God shall wipe away all the tears, sorrow, crying, and pain, indicating that we will be free of any defects or abnormalities.

Dr. Eich explains his ideas concerning this question beautifully. First, he believes we will be *functionally* made whole in heaven. That means we will be able to *do* everything that we need to do. Also, we will be structurally perfect, in that those who are blind will be able to see, those who are deaf will be able to hear, and so on. But there is one exception. Those whose physical disabilities were a means of grace for them, *or for others*, may have the marks of these means of grace left just as Jesus (after the resurrection) still had holes in his hands and feet. Thus, Damien may still show scars of his leprosy, Stephen may have bruises from the stones, and the spina bifida child may show signs of his defect. But, these scars will not be painful, will not interfere with function, and will not be ugly (in fact, they will seem beautiful to us, because they were a means by which God's grace was shown to us).

My little girl, Haley, was a trisomy-18, so she may show physical signs of her condition. However, she will be functionally normal, so the signs will be beautiful to me because I will *finally* be able to see how God used her disability to teach me how to love more. Actually, Haley was beautiful to me here on earth. I always felt drawn to her and that she was so perfect in the midst of all her disorders. Looking at her was like seeing a piece of heaven. Maybe that is why I felt a little closer to heaven while she was alive!

4. Do babies have to live on earth before they can enter heaven? (This particular question seems to bother mothers of miscarried and stillborn babies.)

There *must* be children in heaven. My personal belief concerning whether unborn children enter heaven is that if it is very important to the parents to see and know their child in heaven, God will make it so. Although God's ways seem strange sometimes, I do believe His ways in heaven will be very clear. I also believe He will allow us to be happy with our loved ones, especially ones that are very dear and important to us. And, after all, who could be more important than our own children? Heaven would not be heaven to me without seeing Haley there.

My mother's immediate response to this question of children in heaven was, "That is a senseless question, because children come from heaven; so, why should they not be allowed to enter heaven when they die?" Just touching, holding, smelling, and loving a baby makes a person realize that a baby is created by an all-powerful God who would certainly want such a special part of heaven back again. In Psalms 139:13–15, it is made clear that God does know us even as we form in the womb. Also, in Jeremiah 1:5, God tells Jeremiah "before I formed thee in the belly I knew thee." These passages suggest that God does know babies in heaven, even before He sends them to us on earth.

Dr. Hudson Baggett, editor of the *Alabama Baptist*, is very explicit and to the point on the subject. He said, "It is my feeling that life begins at conception, and this is sufficient to say that a person has lived." His statement should be a very comforting thought for mothers of miscarried and stillborn babies.

According to Dr. Eich, it is thought that about 50 percent of all human pregnancies end in spontaneous abortion. If the soul enters the child at conception, then this indicates that at least one-half of heaven's population would consist of the souls of unborn children. To some people, this would surely seem excessive, but God may not be very *thrifty*. He may like having a great number of children there! After having my children, I can certainly understand His reasoning!

5. Is it God's will for my baby to die?

I do not believe it is God's will for a baby to die. The God I believe in would never purposely *will* such tragedy and pain. The common theory is that God *allows* these things to happen. This theory bothers me because if God could prevent this tragedy and chooses not to, that is contradictory to His nature. Why would a merciful God *allow* such intense suffering and pain? I want Him to have the power to control everything; but, I do not want to believe He would choose to let my baby suffer and die and cause me to hurt so intensely.

I like to think that God is all-powerful, merciful, and caring. I do believe He can do anything, although I question why little children have to suffer in the process. I think He is merciful in that He constructed me in such a manner that I could survive my loss successfully. I want to believe He cares for me and that He has some reason for allowing bad things to happen to people. I am sure God does not tell us why He allows evil, because we are not capable of understanding the answer. Sometimes, I wonder if I really want to understand why my little girl died. An acceptable answer almost seems callous. In Job 38—39, God's real message to Job was that we could not understand the answer to "why?" In essence, He is saying that until we have made a universe, known the place where rain is stored, set stars and suns spinning in motion, and cradled humanity in the palm of our hand, we cannot understand the reason that people suffer.

Leslie Weatherhead, a British Methodist theologian, places God's will into three distinct categories. They are as follows:

I. God's intentional will;
II. God's circumstantial will;
III. God's ultimate will.

God's *intentional will* is that which He had in mind at creation. The Bible makes it clear that God's intent was that man live in paradise in the garden of Eden with no suffering or pain. In the same way, I am sure God intended for chromosomes always to line up and distribute normally, for all babies to be fully and normally developed, and for all of us to live happy, untarnished lives. But, for some reason, He allows errors and suffering to occur. Most theologians believe that nature is flawed because of Satan's rebellion and/or Adam's sin. These flaws were not God's will, but, for some unknown reason, He allows them to exist.

God's *circumstantial will* is the will of God in a particular, actual situation. It differs from the intentional will, in that evil has already entered the situation in many cases. For example,

God's will may well be served when a dangerous criminal is punished accordingly by society. The evil exists in the crime that was committed, and God's circumstantial will is applied through appropriate punishment or when justice is served.

God's intentional will is that all children be born normal. But, sickness and death entered the world through Adam's sin and/or the rebellion of Satan and his angels. God has allowed suffering and evil to exist in the universe since that time. We do not know why. Dr. Eich thinks perhaps God respects their quasi-legal right to do their satanic thing, until such time as the creation comes to its end. Any child's defect or suffering is the result of Satan's work, making creation imperfect. Of course, an imperfect creation was not God's original intention, but God permits its existence.

God's *ultimate will* occurs when God enters a situation, which has deviated from His intentional will. He then *redeems* the situation so that sometimes good can come from it. For example, my little girl was born with a genetic defect; so, God entered into the situation and willed for it to serve a purpose. Understand, God did not make her have the defect in order to accomplish His purpose, but, once she had the defect, He redeemed and continues to redeem the evil by using the defect to accomplish good. This was a hard concept for me to comprehend at first, because my shattering hurt was all-consuming, and I did not have room in my heart and mind for anything else but pain. I could not see any good in all the pain and suffering that occurred because of Haley's defect. Now, with a little time and a lot of reestablishment, I have worked for a positive, fulfilling purpose for Haley's suffering and death. As Dr. Eich states, "The devil may win a skirmish or two; but, ultimately, God always emerges as the victor." I believe the good that has resulted from Haley's suffering and death has taken form in the writing of this book, which is a means of growth for me and, I hope, a means of healing for others.

6. God will not give people more grief than they can bear.

I feel this statement is terribly overrated. People who have lost a child do not like to be told this, especially by someone who does not know the depth of their loss and pain. When I had my little girl and was told she would die, I personally felt that if the statement "God will not give you more than you can bear" was true, then God surely had overestimated my strength! Also, I have known some very fine, religious, strong people who have been totally broken by tragedies in their lives, leading me to believe that some people do get more than their share of trouble and suffering; as a result, it does prove to be more than they can bear.

I see people who have a lot more on them than I feel *I* could bear; yet, I would have never thought that I could bear the loss of my little girl. Fortunately, I have been able to sort my way through my loss and reestablish myself. I take great pride in the fact that I have indeed been able to bear my heartbreaking burden; but, I also feel that I have had my share of pain for this lifetime. I do believe a person can take just so much, and then the damage becomes irreversible. I must admit, at the time Haley died, I would not have given a cent for my odds of being truly happy again; so I feel God did not put on me more than I could bear *this* time. However, I certainly do not want Him to ask me to deal with more. I might *survive* more tragedy, in that I would be *alive*, but the question would become, "What would my quality of life be?" I feel that some people can bear more than others, and that we can safely assume that God gives us strength, but whether strength is enough is open to question. Dr. Eich believes that God will not put more on a person than that person and his *support system* can handle, provided he take advantage of the opportunities to develop his support system, which may mean a church, a support group such as A.M.E.N.D., a group of friends, or a psychotherapy relationship. Naaman Goode, a Church of Christ minister, refers to I Corinthians 10:13, which states that God will provide a way of escape, so we can bear any burden. This escape can easily be the support system to which Dr. Eich refers.

Any tragedy is hard to bear and requires a lot of personal effort to survive the intense pain and emptiness, but I believe it can be done. The question is, "Do you have the strength to search out the way for you to bear the loss?" It is not a sign of weakness to need outside help; in fact, it is a sign of maturity and intelligence to recognize the need for such help. Actually, it is a definite sign of strength to seek and get the help that you need.

7. Our children are really God's first, and He is simply sharing them with us for a while.

The implication of this commonly quoted statement is that we should not get angry or hurt when God chooses to take back something that is already His. On one level this is true, since we do, indeed, hold our children in trust. Brother Goode refers to Ezekiel 18:4: All creation is God's and all souls belong to God. But, on another level, because we grow to love our children, this thought from the scripture does not keep it from hurting any less if we lose them.

The problem, of course, is that parents are human, and humans do attach themselves to their children. Thus, it hurts overwhelmingly when our children die. A mother bonds with a child even before birth, because the baby is a part of her being. I am sure foster parents can identify with this feeling of attachment to a degree, but they know to try *not* to get attached. They also know the child is still alive and happy when they do give him up to be adopted. Parents of children who die do not have this luxury. All they have in their minds are the cold, hard facts of death.

According to Dr. Eich, the Jews tell a story about a rabbi who had two sons. They were the apple of his eye, and he adored them more than anything. One day, while the father was out, the sons died. When the father returned, his wife asked, "Suppose a friend left two precious gems for you to keep and enjoy until he needed them again. When he returned and asked for them back, would you begrudge his taking them?" "Of course not!" he replied. "Then come with me and see what has happened," she said, as she took him to see his two boys.

The only problem with this little story is that two gems cannot be compared to two children. Two gems I can give up, but the life of my child cannot be measured by any means known to man as far as I am concerned. The parental instincts are from God, and the love is from God. Therefore, the pain of loss is very real. The story has a nice thought, but it does not eliminate the hurt for me. All this means is that people can say all the words in the world or tell all the well-meaning stories, but the hurt . . . the all-consuming pain . . . will still be there.

8. Is it all right to be angry with God, and will He punish us for doubting His wisdom?

Anger, which is defined by Webster as "a strong feeling of displeasure," is almost always present when parents lose a child. The anger may be vented in many ways and toward different people. However, it usually ends up being directed toward God also. Many times, parents will deny anger toward God simply out of the fear of His wrath. Dr. Eich warns, "If you *pretend not* to be angry, the anger just festers and makes psychological pus. Psychologically, it is much better to let the pus drain out, by recognizing the anger and expressing it. God understands that."

I believe it is much more dangerous to our relationship with God to *pretend* the anger does not exist, than it is to recognize it and express it. After all, God knows how we *really* feel anyway, and He can take the anger along with our honest expression of it. If people deny or repress their anger, it can destroy a relationship. I believe you must recognize the anger, accept it, and then ask God for help in dealing with it. A friend of mine told me, "God *uses* life's *bruises*." I believe this, and I also believe that a person's relationship with God may actually grow deeper and more meaningful because of the bruises. I will never forget talking with my own minister about my anger. I was afraid that he might not want to speak at my daughter's funeral if he knew how I really felt, but I also knew that I owed him an honest appraisal of my feelings concerning God. I felt so good after admitting and venting my anger to him. His answer was simply, "I would have thought you a liar if you had told me you were not angry with God. I think you will be all right."

One of my sources, Brother Goode, believes that to be angry with God and doubt His wisdom is to show a lack of faith. I strongly disagree with this opinion, because I have known and heard of many fine Christian people who have shown displeasure with God. For example, once Saint Theresa, of Avila, was boating with two other nuns. A sudden wave or wind overturned the boat. Saint Theresa came up sputtering, shook her fist at heaven, and screamed, "If you treat your friends like this, it's no wonder you have so few!" She was a very holy woman who lived close to God; but, she was not afraid to let Him know when she was angry with Him. It was a childish tantrum, of course, but then she never claimed to be anything but a child of God! Dr. Eich sums it up beautifully: "A wise and loving father does not punish his children for being children; and, a wise and loving God does not punish His children for being human."

9: *"Ask and ye shall be given. Seek and ye shall find." Why didn't God give me a healthy baby? I prayed for my baby to be normal.*

I do believe God listens to our prayers, but I also realize that His answers are not always exactly what we had in mind. Some of the things people ask for obviously would be out of line, such as praying for a diamond ring or an airplane. Nevertheless, it is certainly all right to pray for obviously good things, like a healthy baby. Brother Goode says, "God does answer our prayers. His answers can be: (a) yes, (b) no, (c) wait a while, or (d) I will give you something better. Just as an earthly father does not give a child everything that the child asks for, neither does the heavenly Father grant every request made of Him." I can accept the answer "no" for unworthy prayer requests, but it is very hard to understand "no" to the prayer for a healthy baby.

If we could compel God to do what we want, simply by asking Him for it, then He would not be God. He would be a genie in a bottle, according to Dr. Eich. If we got everything we wanted, we would be in heaven, not on earth. This is earth, not heaven; therefore, a certain amount of evil exists. Unfortunately, this evil takes form periodically by causing defects in our children, causing them to suffer and/or die.

10. Is God just and fair?

God is just and fair, but many of the circumstances of life do not *seem* to be just and fair. In other words, God is just and fair in the things that *He does*; the seemingly unfair defect and/or death of a baby is caused by the random evil in the world and not by the will of God. This randomness seems to indicate fairness, in that He does not single out good people, bad people, poor people, rich people, short people, tall people, old people, or young people. Bad things seem to occur to all kinds and groups of people. So, I choose to believe that God, *in His final judgments*, is just and fair. Although it is not clear to me why God tolerates these random flaws of nature to exist, I hold on to the belief that He will make it all perfectly clear and acceptable at the time He chooses to end our earthly existence.

11. If God knows everything and is all-powerful, then why did He let my baby die? Why couldn't He figure out another way to accomplish His purpose?

I do not know for sure what God's purpose was in my daughter's suffering and death, but I do know what things have resulted from her death. For example, I am sure that I would not be writing this book if she had not died; I am certainly a better mother, wife, daughter, and all-around person than I would have been if Haley had not entered my life; I am more gentle, more tactful, more sympathetic, more understanding, more patient, and certainly stronger as a result of her death. All of these things are a direct result of my pain. I am sure these gains would *not* exist to the degree they do without my daughter's death, and I am also just as sure these gains have come *only* through my loss. There is nothing known to me that could possibly touch me to the degree that my baby's death has. I want God's purpose to be overwhelmingly great, because the heartache and devastating pain have been too much for the purpose to be small and simple.

I believe that God is all-powerful, that He has vast knowledge, and that He will clear up my *misunderstanding* of Haley's death and my pain someday. For now, I choose to trust that Haley's death will continue to be for a wonderful purpose. Thus, I will continuously strive to make positive things happen as a result of her death and my loss.

12. God is not asking more from me than He asked from Himself. He gave His son, so I should be willing to give my child.

This, believe it or not, is a common statement made to mothers who have lost a child. Obviously, the mother of a dead child does not feel the circumstances are quite the same, in that her child's death will not save the world. This statement comes from people who really do not understand the depth of sorrow that the mother of a sick and/or dying infant feels. A child's sickness, suffering, and death have absolutely no relation to God's sacrifice of His son, other than God's parallel understanding of our loss. Our children suffer disease and death, because we live in a world of sin.

God is somewhat of a fellow sufferer. Yet, He fully understood the purpose in His loss, whereas we do not have the luxury of that understanding. We have to survive on faith. I feel all our inequities will be righted in the judgment.

13. Why innocent children?

It bothers me greatly to know innocent children have to sometimes suffer the pains of earthly existence. The Bible makes it very clear that children are truly *special* to God. This specialness is pointed out in Matthew 18:1–10, a beautiful reference to God's special feelings and high regard for our children. The Bible says we will have to be as children to enter the kingdom of God, and that our children will have special positions in God's kingdom, where they can always see the face of God. Mark 10:3-16 points out that innocent children are safe, for such is the kingdom of God. Brother Goode makes a very good point by saying, "Don't feel sad for a child that has gone to be with God and has not had to suffer the trials and tribulations of this life."

Conclusion

I have done a great deal of reading in the Bible since Haley's death, and I have heard many opinions concerning the death of children. I do believe that the Bible *represents* the word of God, in that it was written by men inspired by God. The writers' vocabulary styles and the personal peculiarities of their cultures and time are all evident in the scriptures. I also feel that modern translations may change or alter some areas of thought, as to apply more readily to our present day vocabulary styles and cultural peculiarities. I believe the Bible is God's revelation of Himself to man; therefore, I accept the Bible as inspired, authoritative truth. With all of this in mind, I find great comfort in the answers, scriptures, translations, ideas, and opinions that I have revealed throughout this topic concerning God's role in our losses.

6

The Aftershock of Death

There are several stages of grief, according to Peppers, Knapp, and Ross (the writers of *Motherhood and Mourning* and *Death, the Final Stage of Growth*). These stages are: (1) shock, (2) disorganization, (3) volatile emotions, (4) guilt, (5) loss and loneliness, (6) relief and reestablishment, and (7) shadow grief. As you progress through the stages, you will experience several feelings and thoughts that will possibly frighten you or, at the very least, be very unsettling. Most of these feelings and thoughts are normal, even though they may seem crazy at the time. The main thing is to accept that these thoughts and feelings exist and that they are perfectly normal and acceptable as a part of the grieving process. I am going to share several normal behaviors, thoughts, and feelings that often occur with grieving parents who have lost their child. Keep in mind that, as crazy or irrational as some of these things may seem, they are, indeed, perfectly normal behavior for bereaved parents.

1. Reading the Obituaries

Most young people and adults do not think about reading the obituaries until their child dies. In general, people consider the obituaries for older people. Almost unexpectedly, I read the "CREEL INFANT" in the obituaries, and it made me realize that babies do die. After Haley's death, I found myself, instead of going directly for the comic section, the sports, or Ann Landers, going immediately to the obituaries each day. I would quickly scan to see if any infants had died. I would wonder about the families and circumstances involved. This is all perfectly normal, and it will probably persist any length of time, from several months to many years. The intensity of feelings and thoughts that occur when reading the obituaries will mellow with time.

2. Raw Feelings

Bereaved parents' feelings will get hurt very easily. This is very logical, if you give it some thought. There are days, under normal circumstances, that you are more sensitive than other days. When your child dies, your feelings are stretched beyond their limit, and little things just become too much to handle at times. You may have difficulty concentrating, and you may be vulnerable to insensitive small talk that you would usually think nothing about. Such reactions will pass with time, and you will actually begin to "remember when" such trite statements or actions used to bother you. You will actually be proud that you have progressed beyond that point.

3. Other Babies and Children

Other peoples' babies have different effects on grieving parents. Some bereaved parents do not like to be around another baby, because the baby is a painful reminder of their dead child. Another baby may simply intensify the loss and may cause the grieving parents to lose control, to the point of crying or expressing anger. These reactions cause uncomfortable feelings among everyone involved.

On the other hand, some grieving parents may long to hold and touch other babies. They may have fleeting thoughts of stealing a baby when they see one out in public, or they may have fantasies about a baby when they see and hold other children. I can remember sitting in the waiting room at my

So, to some parents, it is actually comforting to go to the cemetery, and to others it is much too painful and unsettling.

7. *Conditioned Reflexes*

Some examples of conditioned reflexes are phantom crying, aching arms syndrome, aching breasts syndrome, and activation of routine tasks concerning the baby. We condition ourselves to these reactions, by anticipating the routines of a baby while we are pregnant; or, if we take a baby home before he dies, we are conditioned by things we do in caring for the child.

I remember, after Haley died, I would periodically think I heard her cry. I would catch myself running toward the den to check on her, and then I would remember . . . she could not be crying. At first I was afraid everyone would think I was insane, so I did not tell anyone. One day, while my husband, two sons, and I were eating dinner, I thought I heard Haley cry in the den. I tried to keep my thought to myself. But Austin, my younger son, said, "I thought I heard Haley cry," and Kevin, my older son, remarked that he heard it also; and then Larry and I both, in unison, said "I thought I heard her too." What a relief! I felt better knowing we all were hearing the phantom crying. Of course, I think it was really unusual that we all heard it at the same time.

The aching arms and breasts syndromes are very common for mothers. My arms would literally ache to hold and rock my baby. I would go to Haley's room and rock stuffed toys or her newborn picture, while I closed my eyes, cried, and dreamed of holding and rocking Haley. My breasts ached deeply to nurse Haley. As hard as I tried, she simply never had the strength to nurse. I wanted to breastfeed so badly, because I felt it might help her survive.

Activation of routine tasks occurs with bereaved parents who have taken care of their baby at home. Obviously, when parents take a baby home, they quickly fall into a routine of taking care of the child. This routine will probably include such child has died. They may catch themselves laughing or enjoying themselves, then they will withdraw because of guilty feelings.

6. *Visiting the Cemetery*

Some parents need to go to the cemetery periodically, and some absolutely cannot go. The parents who go to the cemetery regularly, go for several reasons. They go to keep the little grave and marker clean; they go to visit with their baby in spirit; they go to dream of what could have been; they go to cry and vent their pain; they take their other children to show them that they would never be forgotten and left alone if they were to die also (it is important to eliminate the fear of abandonment for other surviving children); and they go to protect the grave. The first rain usually bothers the parents, and some will find themselves out at the cemetery with their umbrella over the grave. The parents usually know it is futile, but they feel they have to try. I can remember trying to keep Haley's grave dry with my body, because I did not have my umbrella with me. I begged God to stop the rain. Of course, I got soaked and gave up, but trying to protect the grave while yelling at God made me feel better.

Another form of protection was cleaning bird droppings off the marker. It infuriated me beyond measure that a bird would have the degrading audacity to release droppings on my little girl's grave and marker. I wanted to sit out there and shoot the birds until they all were dead, to punish them for their unforgivable deed. I realize now that the birds do not mean to dirty Haley's marker as a personal vendetta but I still do not particularly care for their untimely release. Also, I still stamp and destroy ants and their hills if they make the mistake of choosing to build on Haley's grave.

Many parents do not feel a need to go to the cemetery; in fact, they may feel compelled to totally avoid the cemetery. They simply cannot deal with the bare dirt and finality of the little grave that represents broken hearts, empty arms, and unfulfilled dreams.

a pregnant woman. They actually fear what may be in store for the prospective mother. I can remember when I would see a pregnant woman at the mall and I would think how terrible it would be if her baby died or had a defect. I would actually feel hurt over the possibility that she might have to suffer as I had suffered.

Another normal feeling is simple irritation that someone else is pregnant and everything seems fine; whereas, the grieving parents had to go through such seemingly unnecessary and unwarranted pain because of their loss. The pregnant woman represents the state of happy, forthcoming joy because the state of pregnancy seems to be safe in that nothing bad occurs until the baby is delivered as dead or defective. I think bereaved parents may feel as if they may never experience this safe state again.

5. *Happiness*

At first, it irritated me to be around happy people. I did not really want people to be as unhappy and sad as I was, but it did hurt that others could be happy and I could not. I just wanted to be as happy as everyone else. I honestly wondered if I could ever be truly happy again. I remember that even happy television commercials irritated me; the baby product commercials and happy family commercial settings were very painful to watch. I realized the world had a right to go on its merry way; but, that did not keep me from hurting. I think these happy situations provoked feelings of jealousy, despair, and a fear of losing my happiness forever.

I did not really like unhappy people either. I felt that they were unhappy over little, meaningless things, and that they should be thankful they did not have a dead baby. I wanted to tell them they did not know what real unhappiness was and that they had no right to be unhappy over trite things. I guess I felt as if I had cornered the market on misery!

Also, some grieving parents feel guilty if they have fun. They feel as if they should not enjoy anything, because their doctor's office, seeing other mothers with their newborns, and wanting to touch the little ruffles, feet, or hands of the baby. I would want to ask to touch or hold the baby, but I was always afraid I might cry or that the mother really would not want some stranger touching her baby. Oh . . . how I longed to have my little girl in my arms again! When I did have the pleasure of holding another person's baby, I had such conflicting emotions. It hurt so deeply; but, it also was so wonderful, soft, warm, and pleasing just to have a baby in my arms again.

I can also remember resenting other parents with babies, if I felt they were not taking care of their child as I would. For example, it would anger me to see a bedraggled, unkempt child with a dirty face, tangled hair, and stained or ragged clothing, because I always felt I would care enough to take better care of *my* baby. In turn, when I saw a little girl who had sweet little ruffles and a pretty bow in her hair, I would immediately think, *That's just how I would have Haley look and dress if she were alive.*

Another thing that might trouble parents is to see children grow up that were born near the same time as their baby. They may think, *I wonder what my baby would have looked like on his first birthday . . . or seventeenth birthday.* Parents may also find themselves shopping for clothes that would fit their child, as if he were growing up. But, I find that I still look at dresses for a newborn, because I really cannot imagine Haley being two years old and me shopping for 2T dresses.

I am sure there may be parallel and conflicting feelings concerning other children for quite a while after your baby dies.

4. Other Pregnant Women

Other pregnant women bring out an assortment of emotions for grieving parents. Some bereaved parents hate seeing pregnant women, because it makes the parents feel envious and inadequate. There even may be fleeting thoughts of animosity. Other grieving parents feel such emotions as pity or sorrow for was wrong, and I did not react as I thought I would. For example, I had a friend who had three miscarriages before she ever successfully carried a baby. Each time, I told her it was for the best and that surely she did not want an unhealthy, sick, or deformed baby instead of losing it. I could not understand how she could be so upset over such a loss. SHAME ON ME! Since that time, I have had a miscarriage, and it was a horrible experience. I felt such emptiness and worthlessness. I felt that I could not even do what was natural and normal for a woman: to carry a baby to term. But, it took my loss to make me realize how much a miscarriage could affect a mother. Never underestimate the pain of the loss of a baby, even if it is a miscarriage. The first thing I did after I recovered from the physical aspect of the miscarriage was to call my friend, tell her how sorry I was that I had not been more understanding, and also to ask for her help and understanding to get me over my loss. She was very helpful, and she offered a shoulder to cry on. Thankfully, she was a better friend to me than I had been to her.

Babies lost before term (stillborn, miscarriage) carry the deep hurt of unfulfilled dreams and the loss of a much wanted child. The parents will suffer from the lack of memories rather than having memories to pull them through. They are basically left with nothing to hold onto except emptiness and failure. The parents are faced with direct and indirect reminders of their loss daily. They see pregnant women; they see and hear about friends and family members with newborns; and, they see little clothes, the empty nursery, the empty arms, and the empty heart. To add to the pain, if it was a first baby, they will also fear not being able to have other children. As a friend, do not wear yourself out trying to understand, but, instead, just be a good friend. Be there to cry with, talk with, remember with, and, above all, to care with the parents.

Another gesture toward comforting the parents would be a written note or card. I remember getting beautiful, comforting notes and cards for about three months after Haley died and each personal note meant so much. I remember one note from a colleague that really touched my heart. I can remember pulling the note out periodically and reading it, just to draw strength to get through many rough moments. A personal note or card is a meaningful and savable gesture. It made me feel good to see the box full of notes, showing me that other people really did care and recognize my sorrow.

Another wonderful gesture is to donate a book in memory of the child, or to give money to an appropriate fund in the name of the baby. Such an action offers something lasting for the parents to cling to.

Above all else, do not give up on the parents. They should be given room to grow, breathe, and resolve their loss; but, you should always be within calling range. If you do not keep in touch, they may move in the direction of isolation and disorientation. The main thing is to follow your heart, and you will be a true comfort to someone who has lost his child. A feeling is not a waste of time when you feel it in your heart. Let the parents know you feel for what they have been through and for what they will go through. Good friends should be willing to come and willing to listen.

I want to share one of my very dear friends with you. Her name is Diane. Diane had a very uncommon depth of sensitivity to my grief. She has never lost a child, and yet, she seemed to truly feel deeply about my child's death. She has always been willing to listen and be with me during all of my difficult times. I am sure she got tired of hearing the painful words and thoughts I said to her over and over. Fortunately, she let me express my feelings, and she would listen attentively. She cared enough to sit with me all day during the three days I stayed in the hospital after Haley was born. She talked with me, cried with me, and held me, just to let me know she cared. I can still see her face and tears as she hugged me and told me how sorry she was about Haley. She cried and said, "I guess I'm not much help, but I hurt so badly for you, and I don't know what to say or do." I told her

I was so glad to have such a good friend, and we both could just cry together. I needed someone just like Diane to let me cry. I knew she could accept my tears, whereas my own family needed me to be strong. Diane allowed me to have an outlet to vent my feelings, and I felt comfortable with her. The thing that makes Diane so special is that she never *had* to be there or listen to my anger and tears, but she *was* there because she chose to be.

The sadness of losing a baby does not always occur during the daytime. As a matter of fact, much of the intense pain occurs at night, when you are alone or when everyone else is asleep. This brings me to Becky. She is one of my friends that I could call any time, day or night. I woke Becky many mornings as early as one or two o'clock, and, fortunately, she did not hang up on me! My husband travels sometimes, and I would get lonely and start thinking about Haley when he was gone. One thought would follow another, and pretty soon I would work myself into a state of hysteria. So, I would call Becky, and she would listen and then give me words of encouragement.

The reason I wanted to share Diane and Becky with you is because I wanted to point out that you do not have to lose a child to be a good friend to anyone who has lost a baby. The ingredients that go into being a good friend are love, care, sincerity, sensitivity, and a willingness to listen. Be a good friend, and you will make a big difference in someone's life. Who knows . . . *you* may need a good friend someday!

8

Well-meaning People Who Say and Do the Wrong Things

Different people have different needs, but, from all I have ever known and experienced, there are some things you should *not* say to parents who have lost a child. The problem is that people who have never experienced such a loss simply cannot comprehend the depth of sorrow, grief, and suffering the parents are feeling. Because of this lack of understanding people really do not know what to say or do to help grieving parents. Some people will *luck out* and say the right thing at the right time; but, many people will actually offend the grieving parents with some thoughtless cliché.

The hurtful sayings, clichés, or phrases can be avoided, if people will take the time to give some thought to what they say and use their common sense. There are some simple rules to follow that may keep people from putting their feet in their mouths and also hopefully, will spare the grieving parents added anxiety.

1. Do not call or refer to the baby as "it," because this implies the child was nothing more than an inanimate object, rather than a beautiful little baby. If the baby had a name, refer to the child by his/her name. If the baby had not been named, refer to the child as "your baby" because the word "your" gives warmth,

worth, and a feeling of belonging to the child's existence. This reference is profoundly important to the parents.

2. Do not overwhelm the parents with your experiences of grief, such as when your uncle or grandmother died. They are too involved in their own loss to take in yours as well. If you want to comfort them in their loss, do not exploit your problems. At this particular time, the parents cannot cope with anything more than their own pain.

3. If you have a child or newborn, do not try to "share" your child with the parents who have lost a baby. As a matter of fact, it may be best not to expose the bereaved parents to your children for a while. The children may be painful, vivid reminders of their loss.

4. Do not go around the world to avoid the subject of the dead baby. Grief needs to be heard and usually the parents (especially the mother) need to talk about their baby. If they show you pictures, try to point out something positive about the baby, such as "She really had pretty hair," or "He had such perfect little ears." I remember showing Haley's baby picture to a friend who, a couple of days later, gave me the most beautiful, etched brass frame for the picture. It was the perfect gift because I knew she realized how important Haley's picture was to me. It was the perfect frame for a precious picture of *my* beautiful little girl. Seriously, such a gesture means the world to the mother and father. Remember, the baby was a special little person to the parents and acknowledging the baby truly pleases them.

5. Do not be overly curious and nosey. If the parents want to share certain facts and feelings with you, they will, in their own time and way. Do not badger the parents because it will only cause more pain where enough already exists.

6. Do not make flippant statements that might cause more anxiety and stress for the bereaved parents. Some common thoughtless statements that should *not* be used are as follows:

"I know just how you feel."
This remark makes the parents feel as if you are minimizing their loss by comparing it to little disappointments in your life. If you have not experienced losing a child, then do not pretend to understand what the parents are going through. You can sympathize, but do not pretend to empathize.

"This is for the best."
The parents will think, "The best for whom or what?" At this point, they cannot see how the death of their child is the *best* thing. To them, it is the most horrible thing that has ever happened.

"Time will heal everything; you will see."
Although this statement has a lot of truth in it, it does not help. The parents wonder, "How much time?" or "How do you know?" or "No, I am afraid time will not help at all," or even, "What if we cannot make it that long?" You cannot tell them how long it will take for them to feel better, and they do not need the added anxiety of all the other questions that will come to their minds as a result of this cliché. Also, this statement implies that the dead child will not always be important to the parents and that he will fade out of their lives. This thought can be agony to the grieving parents.

"How are you?"
This is an insensitive question. You should realize the parents are miserable, unhappy, devastated, overwhelmingly confused.... Should I go on? Do you expect them to say "Fine!" or candidly remark, "Oh, quite devastated, thank you"?

"Forget about all of this, and think of all the good things in your life."
How can parents just simply forget about their dead baby? Parents do not need to *forget* it; they need to *deal* with the loss.

All the good things in their lives are not the issues here. The pain, loss, and emptiness are the issues. So, do not tell parents to forget such an important part of their lives.

"Oh, I was so sorry to hear about your bad luck."

This statement is careless. BAD LUCK! That is when a senior in high school gets a pimple right before the prom! Or, when your car has a flat tire on a deserted road and it is pouring down rain! The parents feel that their child's death is much more than simply bad luck. Please acknowledge the loss with more depth.

"Surely you are not going to have another baby. What if it dies too?"

First of all, no one has the right to make the decision to have or not to have another baby, except the parents involved. You should never make such a judgment, especially if the parents have not asked for your opinion. Hopefully, the parents will research their options thoroughly before they make their decision concerning another child. They certainly do not need your thoughtless, shallow remarks, and they definitely do not need your disapproval.

"This is God's will."

I believe this is one of the most common statements made to parents who have lost a child and it is probably one of the hardest for them to hear. I just hated to be told my daughter's illness and death were God's will. It made me feel as if God had betrayed me. Parents need to feel supported by God, not betrayed by Him. I believe God *allows* these tragedies to be a part of our lives, but I certainly do not feel He *wills* such pain. It is best to keep such callous statements to yourself.

"You are actually lucky. . . . It could be worse."

LUCKY! Lucky is when you win the million-dollar lottery, not when your child dies. Even if things could be worse, the parents do not care. All they know is the worst thing in *their* lives has happened. . . . Their child is dead. They hurt so much that nothing else matters. Do not be heartless and tell them how *lucky* they are. Instead, recognize their hurt as real.

"God needs another little angel in heaven" or *"Now you have a little angel in heaven."*

The parents do not need these little poetic thoughts and statements. Such remarks seem trite and tactless to them. The parents do not want a little angel in heaven; they want a baby at home with them.

"Your child is better off this way."

This statement implies that the grieving parents should be *glad* because of the child's death and release from this painful earthly life, and that they are selfish to want him back. The parents know the child is better off not suffering, but this fact does not eliminate their consuming loss, loneliness, and emptiness. Although they are relieved that their baby does not have to suffer, they still have such excruciating pain because of their loss. Bereaved parents have a right to hurt, and they should be allowed to express their grief without reservations.

"Aren't your other children enough?" or *"You should be satisfied with the healthy child you already have."*

This statement implies that the parents should not feel a loss because they have other children to fill the emptiness and to take the place of the dead child. Of course, the parents love their other children, but their other children do not change the fact that they have a dead child also. Each child in a family is special, unique, and has his own position in the family unit. The death of a child leaves an empty spot in the lives of all the family members. Therefore, the parents have an irrefutable right to grieve over their loss.

"How do you do it?"
"What choice do we have?" would be the reply to such a remark. The parents have no choice. They either deal with the death or they do not. It is a simple fact of life that people do what they have to do. The parents do it because they have to; so, do not make a statement implying that the parents chose such a task. Believe me, they would never choose to "do it" if they did not have to.

"Be thankful you did not have the baby any longer than you did, because you would have been more attached."
Even if the baby was miscarried, the parents knew about the child long enough to have dreams and plans for a beautiful child. They have lost their future, and this is very painful. When a baby is stillborn or dies shortly after birth, parents still have the bonding of the pregnancy and the devastating halt of their best-laid plans. Do not ask the parents to be thankful for a *lesser* degree of loss, because, no matter how you look at it, they have lost their child. They deserve the right to grieve, and the amount of grief should not be measured.

"Your baby has just gone to sleep."
Do not try to talk down to the parents or treat them like children. They know their baby has died, and it is insulting to imply the baby is merely sleeping. It is much better to come out and acknowledge the death than to pretend it has not happened.

"My mother died five years ago, and it still hurts just as much now as it did then. Believe me, it will not get better."
This statement makes bereaved parents feel hopeless. Do not make them feel any worse than they already do. It is true that *some* people do not get over the loss of a loved one, but *most* people *do* get much better with time and reorganization.

If you are one who still has difficulty dealing with death, please have the decency to spare others your negative opinion and allow them to hope things will get better. Grieving parents certainly do not need to fear that they will *always* be so unhappy, and this statement is one that will stay with the parents and cause anxiety and fear. If you cannot be positive, or at least neutral in your remarks, it is best that you say nothing.

"Did you do all you could to save the baby?"

This statement is heartless and totally unacceptable. It implies that the parents should have done more and places such anxiety on their already burdened hearts. They know that they did all they could, but it hurts *beyond measure* for them to think someone believes they did not try hard enough, or that they should have done something more in order to save their baby. The one thing that will help the parents resolve their loss is the knowledge that they did their best. . . . Why take this one positive feeling away from them? If you want to say something along this line, say, "I know you did everything you possibly could. That must be a comfort to you."

Some pointers and ideas as to what is acceptable to say to bereaved parents are as follows:

1. Any response to the parents' grief will depend on the particular situation. Use your common sense in deciding how involved you should get with the details of the child's death.
2. How you say something means everything in conveying your condolences. First of all, present your feelings with depth, sincerity, strength, and meaning. Do not say it halfheartedly; do not act preoccupied with other things; do not act cheery, as though you were at a social event; and do not act rushed, as though you really do not have the time for their loss.
3. Refrain from taxing the bereaved parents with too much talking. This includes too much talk about the illness and/or death of the baby, as well as too much small talk about unre-

lated subjects. You can express your sympathy without talking their ears off! As a matter of fact, if you talk too much, you are much more likely to say something harmful.

4. Friends can be a wonderful source of support and comfort for the grieving parents. Acceptable statements to comfort and support grieving parents in their time of loss would be as follows:

"I am sorry" or *"I care."*

These statements are simple, direct and comprehensive.

"I care for what you are going through and what you will go through."

This statement implies you have given thought to the depth of their loss by saying you know their future is going to be affected by the baby's death. Also, it never hurts to tell someone you care.

"I just wanted you to know I am thinking of you."

This remark lets the parents know you will not forget about their loss as soon as you leave the room. It makes them feel good to know that you consider them in your thoughts.

"I have never experienced what you are going through, but I am sure it must be extremely difficult. Please, know I care and I am thinking of you."

These statements let the parents know you care, you are thinking of them, and you realize, to a limited degree, that they are hurting deeply.

"I do not know what to say or do. I just wanted you to know I care for you."

This comment lets the parents know that, even though you feel awkward with the situation, you still care enough to come to see them. This is 100 percent better than avoiding them and their loss.

"I will continue to pray for you."

This remark implies you have been praying for the parents and you will keep praying for them, even after the funeral is over. This makes the parents feel that you will not forget about them after everything settles down. They need to know you realize it is *not* over after the funeral.

"All the words that I have are completely inadequate to express my feelings for you. I just wish there was something I could say or do to make it better."

Even though you cannot come up with the magic words to make it all better, this comment lets the parents know you would if you could. The statement is thoughtful, expressive, and sensitive to the needs of the parents.

"I hope you can find strength and comfort in knowing that you have a good family and good friends to support you."

This is a thoughtful message that reminds the parents that they have people supporting them who will help them get through their loss.

This next statement has a *limited warranty* because it is acceptable *only* under certain circumstances:

"Call me if you need anything."

Obviously, a casual friend or acquaintance should not make this statement, because he is not close enough to the parents to really mean it. I have listed plenty of things to say; so, avoid this comment unless you are *really* prepared to do *anything* for the bereaved parents. If you do decide to make this offer, say it in a very emphatic, sincere, and strong manner; then, reinforce the statement by saying, "Please . . . call me and I will be there for you. If I do not hear from you, I will call you in a few days and see if you need anything." These added statements give sincerity to the first statement and also let the parents know that you will call to make the offer again. BE SURE TO CALL IF YOU SAY YOU WILL. It is best not to make any offer if you do not actually intend to follow through with it.

There could be more acceptable comments according to the situation, and there could be many other possible combinations of the suggestions listed. The main thing is to give some thought and consideration to any comment that you make. Keep in mind that your goal as a well-meaning friend is to console, support, and comfort the parents. Be a well-meaning person who *says* the *right* things.

The "calm after the storm" is a very good description of the situation after a baby is buried. Many times the parents are overwhelmed with caring people during the hospital experience and at the funeral home and cemetery. It makes the parents feel good to know people care enough to come and support them when their child has died. The time in the hospital, the time at home (if the baby was taken home to die), and the time dealing with the funeral are all full of great activity and tension. Suddenly, it is over . . . for everyone except the bereaved family. What most people do not recognize is that it is not over for the parents. In fact, it is just beginning. The first few weeks and months after the death of the baby are especially difficult. This time is filled with intense grief, loneliness, anger, bitterness, heartache, hopelessness, disorganization, and sadness. Because of these feelings, the parents may become disoriented and isolated. Well-meaning people should realize that the parents will still have tremendous heartache when things settle down after the funeral. The realization of the child's death intensifies and profoundly heightens the excruciating pain of the loss. The finality of the closed casket, all the people leaving, the dirt covering the grave, and the empty house, nursery, and arms will consume the parents with sickening force. This time is when the parents need well-meaning people to help soften the pain by doing a few *simple* things:

1. **Take some initiatives.** You do not have to wait for the grieving parents to ask for something. Be sensitive to the simple needs of the parents. I will never forget when my mother-in-law, at the last minute, hemmed my skirt for Haley's funeral because the store where I purchased the skirt had failed to catch the hem properly. I will never forget the friend who knew I loved plants and also knew I loved everything to be pink for Haley, gave me a beautiful pink violet to keep as a reminder of my little girl. I will never forget the people who brought food for three months after Haley's birth. I never had to cook an entire meal for three solid months. It meant so much to me that people kept on caring.

At first, there are many things going on, and then it all seems to stop. It is as though everyone gets back into a normal routine, and the bereaved parents are still hurting. Wait a week or two, or even a month or so, and take the initiative to fix a meal or send a flower. Such a gesture will mean the world to the parents.

2. **Keep in touch.** Do not avoid the parents because of their loss. A telephone call or a personal note to tell the parents you are thinking of them a few days or weeks after the death is healing and helpful. I remember running out to the mailbox each day, just to see if there were any cards. It thrilled me to know people, even after three to four months, still cared enough to send a personal card or note. It is never too late to send a thoughtful card or note. Believe me, if you are still thinking about the baby's death, you can be sure the parents are still thinking about it.

3. **Be a flexible listener.** Do not make the parents ignore the topics that are filling their minds, just because you feel it might

be awkward or uncomfortable for you. Also, do not make the parents talk about things that they are not quite ready to discuss.

4. **Expect the unexpected.** Be able to roll with the punches. Some days will be "back to normal," and then the very next day may be a difficult one for the bereaved parents. The parents' moods may even change in the course of a few minutes. Do not be surprised if they seem down for no apparent reason. This behavior is completely normal, especially at first.

5. **Remember special dates and events.** It warmed my heart when people called on the one-year anniversary of Haley's death, to tell me they remembered and to acknowledge the fact that I was having a difficult day. You cannot imagine how special such a gesture is to the parents. All it would require is marking your calendar, like you would for any significant date you might want to remember. Of course, the parents of the dead child do not need to mark their calendar, because the date is permanently engraved on their hearts. But, you might put the date down to help you remember to give the parents a call or send them a note. Believe me, it certainly will make their day much easier. Other important days may be the one-week anniversary and the one-month anniversary of the death of the baby. Also, bereaved parents always appreciate a friendly call on any dreary, wet, cloudy, or cold day.

Bereaved parents will never be the same as they were before their child died. This is as it should be. With time and well-meaning friends to help them cope, grieving parents will be fun and wonderful to be around again. They do not need to *know* it all or *understand* it all, but they do need to *bear* it all. A well-meaning person can make all the difference in the lives of bereaved parents. Through all the anger, despair, resentment, sadness, and pain, there is a brightness that can be pulled out *only* by good people who care enough to say and do the *right* things.